FRIENDS

Cowboys, Cattle, Horses, Dogs, Cats, and 'Coons

Other books in the Western Life Series:

Number One: *Catch Rope—The Long Arm of the Cowboy*
by John R. Erickson

Number Two: *Through Time and the Valley*
by John R. Erickson

Number Three: *LZ Cowboy: A Cowboy's Journal 1979—1981*
by John R. Erickson

Number Four: *Panhandle Cowboy*
by John R. Erickson

Number Five: *Some Babies Grow Up To Be Cowboys:
A Collection of Articles and Essays*
by John R. Erickson

FRIENDS

Cowboys, Cattle, Horses, Dogs, Cats, and 'Coons

By
John R. Erickson

Volume 6
Western Life Series

University of North Texas Press
Denton, Texas

Most of the articles in this book appeared first in the author's syndicated newspaper column. The following chapters appeared in slightly different form in *American Cowboy* Magazine: "The Floating Cow," March 1996; "The Phantom Cow," May 1996; part of the material on Frankie McWhorter appeared as an article called "A Loyal Cowdog," October 1996.

All photographs by Kris Erickson

Friends: Cowboys, Cattle, Horses, Dogs, Cats, and 'Coons
is Volume 6 in the Western Life Series

The paper in this book meets the minimum requirements of the American National Standard for Permanence of Paper for Printed Library Materials, Z39.48.1984

Permissions
University of North Texas Press
PO Box 311336
Denton, TX 76203-1336
940-565-2142

Library of Congress Cataloging-in-Publication Data
Erickson, John R., 1943–
    Friends : cowboys, cattle, horses, dogs, cats, and 'coons / John R. Erickson.—1st ed.
        p.   cm. — (Western life series ; no. 6)
    ISBN 1-57441-145-4
    1. Erickson, John R., 1943– —Anecdotes. 2. Cowboy—Texas—Biography—
Anecdotes. 3. Ranch life—Texas—History—20th century—Anecdotes.
4. Erickson, John R., 1943– —Friends and associates—Anecdotes. 5. Animals—
Texas—Anecdotes. 6. Texas—Social life and customs—20th century—Anecdotes.
7. Texas—Biography—Anecdotes. I. Title.
    F391.4 .E75 2002
    976.4'063'092—dc21
                                        2002000648
Design by Angela Schmitt

Table of Contents

Part Five: Horses

Preface

This book is composed of articles I wrote during the 1990s. Some were published in *American Cowboy* magazine and *Livestock Weekly*, and the remainder appeared in a weekly syndicated column that ran in a dozen newspapers in Texas and the West.

What they all have in common is that they deal with the same subject—ranch life as I experienced it in the waning years of the twentieth century. Another theme they share is that each story deals with a particular character that caught my interest. Some of the characters are human, but most are animals—cattle, horses, dogs, cats, and a pet raccoon. The preponderance of animal stories doesn't arise from any prejudice against the human species, but rather from the fact that my line of work, ranching, places me in daily contact with animals, and only occasional contact with human beings.

For want of a better title, I have called this collection *Friends*. These people and animals have been an important part of my life, and to one degree or another, I intruded into theirs.

The reader will notice that I have used the title "Teachers" for the first section of the book. It contains stories about three men who have been special to me and from whom I have learned a great deal, enough so that they should be recognized as my teachers as well as my friends: Ace Reid, Frankie McWhorter, and a cowboy named Andy Samson. Andy Samson wasn't his real name. His life took a tragic turn and I wouldn't feel right about using his name. Those who knew him will recognize him.

I am grateful to the men and animals who have put up with me and loaned me their stories. Without them, I wouldn't have much to write about, for it seems to be my destiny to probe the world of ranching and livestock to find adventure, meaning, and humor.

I am also grateful to Fran Vick, former director of the University of North Texas Press, for giving me an outlet for my tales, and to Kris Erickson, who has been my partner and faithful companion for thirty-three years.

John R. Erickson
M-Cross Ranch
April 2000

Part One

TEACHERS

Ace Reid, "The World's Most Famous Cowboy Cartoonist,"
admiring a wood carving of his character Jake (1984)

Ace Reid

It was a hot day in July 1983. I came home around 4:00 and Kris handed me a telephone message. It said, "Call Ace Reid, Kerrville."

I was shocked. Why would Ace Reid, the famous cartoonist, be calling *me?* I knew him by reputation (everyone in my part of the country knew Ace Reid by reputation) but I had never met him.

I called him at his Kerrville ranch and we talked for maybe a half an hour. He said he had been thinking for a long time about making a trip back to Wichita County, Texas, where he had grown up, to look up old friends and visit places he had known as a kid. He thought it would make a good magazine article, and he wanted me to write it.

"The Old Cowboy Goes Home," he called it, a sorting out of his roots in the country he left in 1952. He told me to think it over for a week and call him back.

I didn't need a week to think about it. I told him it would take me about three days to get my business in order, and then I would leave for Kerrville. I didn't know what to expect when I got there, but I had a feeling that Ace and I would get along just fine.

I threw my business into semi-order, loaded Kris and our three kids in the van, left Jane Friesen in charge of Maverick Books, my publishing company based in Perryton, and off we went to Kerrville.

We packed for a four-day visit. Kris and the children stayed for three weeks and I stayed for two and a half months. I didn't get back to Perryton until the first of October.

I had been right. Ace and I got along beautifully, and after spending a day or so talking with him, I wanted to write a book, not an article. Ace said that was fine with him. I could set up shop in his studio and he would help me in any way he could.

I got to work immediately, conducting hours and hours of interviews with Ace and getting the basic outline of the story. I took handwritten notes at first, then later bought a tape recorder so I could transcribe some of Ace's stories just as he told them.

Since I had brought neither a typewriter nor my computer, the only writing tools I had were a pad and a pen. As my notes began to pile up, and as I got a feeling for the size of the project, I leased a portable computer, set it up in the studio, and began transcribing all my notes and tapes on diskette.

As the weeks passed, the material began to take shape and form, and I got a feeling for the kind of book I wanted to do. It would be the story of Ace's life, based to a large degree on my interviews with him, supplemented by interviews with his family and friends, and by the material in nineteen scrapbooks his wife Madge had kept over the years.

It would be the biography of a living man—indeed, you might even say a living *legend*. I found myself in the enviable position of writing the first book ever done on Ace Reid, at a time when he wanted to look back over his life, when he was around to talk and answer questions, read my early drafts and steer me toward the people I needed to interview.

I considered this a once-in-a-lifetime opportunity, because there was no one in Texas, or anywhere else, to compare with Ace Reid. His kind doesn't come along very often, and to draw a good comparison, you would have to go back to Charlie Russell, Will Rogers, or Mark Twain.

While Ace was known primarily as a cartoonist, the creator of Jake and Maw and the other "Cowpokes" characters that appeared every week in hundreds of papers and magazines, he was much more than that. What many people didn't know about Ace Reid was that he started with nothing but guts and ability, and he and Madge *did everything on their own*. They syndicated his cartoons, brought out his calendars, self-published his books (eleven of them as of 1983), booked his speaking engagements ($1500 a pop), and handled all his promotion and advertising.

What this high school dropout cowboy accomplished in thirty years was amazing. After being told by the major Eastern syndicates that his work wouldn't sell, Ace went out into the small towns from the Rio Grande to the Arctic Circle and became a household word and an artist of the common people.

His books and calendars not only sold, they sold in the millions, and he and Madge did it on their own.

There were times that summer when Ace and I were sitting out on his patio, Ace talking, telling a story as only he could tell it, and I could barely see the outline of his face in the growing darkness. I would find myself thinking, "There he is. I can see him, I can hear him, I can walk over and touch him. But how can I explain what he has done and how he did it?"

I hope the book, *Ace Reid, Cowpoke,* answered those questions, though Ace, like any great man, was ultimately a riddle and a mystery. You can't add up arms and legs and cowboy boots and come out with his accomplishments. You can't deduce Ace's personality from the simplicity of his cartoons.

He wasn't a simple man at all. One minute he could be as guileless as a child, unselfconscious and unaware of his gifts. But a moment later he would make a comment that exhibited shrewdness and psychological depth—enough to let you know that Ace was revealing exactly what he wanted you to see.

One of the questions I had to answer after I had decided to write the book was, who would publish it? It would have made a perfect Maverick Book, and fit right into our line of western humor, but the potential audience for the book was large and I wasn't sure Maverick Books had evolved to the point where we could handle such a big project.

One morning out in Ace's studio, I decided to call my agent at the time, who worked out of New York. I wanted to see what she would say about the Ace Reid book. I picked up the phone and dialed the number. It rang once and I hung up. It suddenly struck me that my agent's first response would be, "I never heard of him."

Over the past ten years, I had wasted a lot of time trying to justify my approach to writing, my subjects, my part of the country to people in New York. I just didn't have the stomach to go through it again with the Ace Reid book.

How do you explain Ace Reid to someone in New York? You don't. You can't.

We would publish *Ace Reid, Cowpoke* through Maverick Books. Whatever we lacked in marketing savvy we would try to make up in enthusiasm, freshness, and a good product.

By the time I left Ace's place in early October, I had the book blocked out into a good working draft, which I would continue to revise over the next six months, all the way through galley proofs. I had done most of my interviewing, research, and writing in two and a half months.

That doesn't sound like much time to spend on a book, but I was working twelve to fourteen hours a day and using the full power of my word processor program to move blocks of text from page to page and chapter to chapter, so I never had to retype anything.

Ace Reid and author John Erickson at the radio station (1985)

We brought out the book in the fall of 1984, a $15.95 hardback, with one of Ace's watercolor paintings on the cover and as many illustrations in the text as we could afford. It told the reader where Ace came from, how and when he set out to become "The World's Most Famous Cowboy Cartoonist" (a title he put after his name back in the 1960s), and what he accomplished.

It wasn't dry reading. It is hard to be solemn about a guy who once walked up to the front desk of an Oklahoma City hotel, pointed to the roller-skating bear at his side, and said, "I need a room for me and my wife." And who rode his horse into a fancy Kerrville cocktail lounge. And who dragged a dead deer into that same lounge, set the beast up on a barstool, and ordered it a martini.

Ace worked hard at being a character, and he *was* a character.

We decided to introduce the book in my hometown of Perryton. We bought Ace a plane ticket to Amarillo, the nearest airport. I met his plane, which turned out to be a big mistake.

The airport was clogged with people, hundreds of them. Ace came off the plane in high spirits. We shook hands and then, in his booming voice, he yelled, "Ladies and gentlemen, I want you to know that this here is John Erickson, a famous author from Perryton!"

People stopped talking and stared at me. I turned purple and stared at the floor. I don't embarrass easily, but Ace had managed to do it. I could have pinched his head off for yelling out my name in front of all those people!

Did that bother Ace? Not one bit. The deeper I blushed, the more he enjoyed it.

On our way out of the airport, I explained that hearing my name yelled in crowded places wasn't something that I enjoyed, and suggested that he not do it again. I should have kept my mouth shut.

Ace said he was hungry, so I drove him over to the Red Barn Steak House, at I-40 and Lakeside Drive. We decided we'd celebrate the new book with a steak dinner, even though I knew in my heart that Ace didn't deserve a good steak, after the shabby trick he'd pulled on me in the airport.

A dry hot dog would have been more appropriate.

We arrived at the Red Barn right at 1:00. The lunch crowd was still there and the place was full. The Red Barn was a big restaurant, and when full, it held a whole bunch of people.

The lady with the menus met us at the door. Ace walked right past her and went out into the middle of the crowded dining room. I knew what was coming, but there wasn't a thing I could do about it.

"Ladies and gentlemen," he bellered, "I want you to meet John Erickson, the world famous author from Perryton! He's just written a new book and you'll probably want to buy a copy!"

Over the years, dozens of Ace's friends had weighed the benefits to mankind of shooting him, but for some odd reason nobody had ever done it. If I had been armed that day, I would have made Madge Reid a widow, right there in the Red Barn.

But I'll have to give Ace credit for one thing. We did manage to sell a few copies of the book in the restaurant.

About six months later, Ace returned to the Panhandle to join me in making an autograph tour. As I recall, we made appearances in Amarillo, Memphis, Pampa, and Borger.

The appearance in Borger was to be held in Edgar Blair's fancy new bank. Ace and Mr. Blair had grown up together during the oil boom days in Electra. The bank's publicity department had arranged for Ace and me to be interviewed on a local radio talk show at 8:00 A.M. The bank did all of its radio advertising on this station, and the people there were excited about the interview. They even ran some spots to promote it.

That morning, we got a late start from Perryton and I exceeded the speed limit on the way to Borger. One of my employees had handled all the arrangements with the Borger bank, and she was supposed to meet us at a certain place and lead us to the station.

Somehow we missed connections. I didn't know the call letters of the station or where it was located, and at five minutes to eight, we were exploring a slum district in Borger, looking for a radio station that I felt sure was over there somewhere.

Ace gazed out the window at all the junk cars sitting up on cinder blocks. "Irkson," he said, "you're just like my wife. You'd rather drive around lost for an hour than to stop and ask somebody for directions. But maybe you'd better."

I pulled into a quick-stop grocery and ran in to ask directions to the nearest radio station. I got the directions, jumped back into the van, and off we went. We roared up in front of the station at 8:05.

I jumped out and ran inside. A young man came out of the control room and greeted me. I handed him a copy of the book and said, "I'm John Erickson and that's Ace Reid. We're supposed to do an interview and we're running a little late."

The man looked at the book and looked at Ace. He walked into an office and talked to another man. I couldn't hear what they were saying. A minute later, he returned and said, "Okay, it'll take me a minute to get set up."

I breathed a sigh of relief. We were late, but at least we hadn't missed the show.

It took the guy a couple of minutes to set up a microphone, and I noticed that he was thumbing through the book. He probably hadn't read it, but that was nothing unusual. After you've done a few publicity tours, you learn that the people who do interviews seldom know anything about the books they're discussing. More than once, I had been introduced as "John Ehrlichman, author of the Frank the Cowboy series of books."

At last the fellow came out of the control room and told us to come in. After such a harum-scarum beginning, the interview went surprisingly well. Even though the interviewer hadn't read the book, it was obvious that he had followed Ace's work over the years and was happy to have such a celebrity on his show. It was a good interview.

That done, Ace and I drove across town to the bank, where people were lined up and waiting for Ace's autograph. We had come close to starting the morning off on a sour note, but heroes that we were we had managed to snatch victory out of the jaws of disaster.

We were met at the front door by a man wearing a business suit and a frown. It was the bank's public relations man. "What happened to the radio interview?" he asked.

I smiled at Ace. "Well, we were a little bit late, but we got it done, and it was a good one too."

The PR man stared at us. "You did an interview on the radio? Today? In Borger?" We nodded. His head sank into the palm of his hand, and he groaned, "*You went to the wrong station!*"

It turned out to be an embarrassment for the bank, but I couldn't help admiring the guy at the station. He had known *exactly* what he was doing. He had stolen a celebrity interview from his competitor, and he'd been so slick about it that we'd never suspected a thing.

Ace loved it. It was exactly the sort of thing he would have done on purpose, if he'd just thought about it.

In public Ace was always loud, funny, outrageous, and larger than life. People who met him never forgot him. That's just the way he planned it. Ace created a public personality for himself in order to be noticed as an artist.

In that he was a brilliant success. When he began his career in the early 1950s, there was no such thing as a "western artist." There was Charlie Russell and Frederick Remington, and the rest of the page was a huge blank.

To succeed as an artist, Ace had to draw a crowd, and to draw a crowd he had to be outrageous.

I saw that side of him many times, and I admired him for using his talents to accomplish his mission as an artist. But I saw another side of him that I preferred to the public man, and that is the Ace I remember most fondly.

I spent a lot of time with him and got to know him rather well. One of the qualities I remember most about Ace was his personal integrity. He lived by a simple code of ethics and I suspect that it came from the ranch people he admired so much.

You didn't need a lawyer with Ace. You wrote your deal down on a napkin, shook hands, and then threw away the napkin. He kept his end, and you'd better keep yours.

There were times when Ace probably should have used a lawyer. He made a few deals on napkins that he should have used to wipe his mouth. Everybody wasn't as honest as he was, and not everyone deserved his trust. But he kept his word with me—and I mean right down to the letter—and in an age when that doesn't mean very much, particularly among public figures, I admired that about him.

Another quality I remember about Ace was his sensitivity. I know, that sounds odd to anyone who ever met him in public—a 230-pound jam box in cowboy clothes, with the volume turned up.

I wouldn't say that Ace was an introspective man, even in private. He was too restless to spend much time examining himself or his inner thoughts. Sometimes he reminded me of a child who could hardly bear for life to proceed at its normal pace. It was always too slow for him. Yet he was a very astute observer of the life around him. I was often astonished by his ability to "read" people. Someone close to Ace once warned me, "Don't ever try to lie to him. When you walk into the room, Ace already knows what you're thinking. He reads a face like a book."

One day Ace and I had lunch in a Kerrville restaurant. Out in the lobby, two young ladies sat on a sofa. Ace went over to them. He had never seen them before.

"How are you girls today?" They said fine. "What's your names?" They told him: Marsha and Linda. Ace spoke to Marsha. "Where do you live?"

"Here in Kerrville."

"Where was you raised?"

"Oh, all around."

"You ain't from Russia, are you?"

The girls stared at each other in disbelief. Then Marsha said, "Why yes! We came to this country ten years ago."

That was typical of Ace Reid—walking up to a total stranger and, within seconds, coming up with an obscure piece of information. Though I had seen him do it before, I was amazed.

Outside, I asked him about it. "Ace, how the heck did you figure out that she was from Russia? You didn't talk to her for more than a minute."

He shrugged and said, "It kind of surprised me too."

Ace told me on several occasions that he had extrasensory perception, and I believed he did.

Ace died in November 1991. I often think of him and remember the time we spent together. There will be other books done on Ace Reid, books written by people better qualified than I to assess his place in the world of art and the impact he has had on his times. But no one will ever have the opportunity I had—to live with him day and night, to watch him draw and play with his dog, and to sit with him on long summer nights, talking about life, death, horses, cowboys, art, and fame.

Ace Reid was a remarkable man. I'm very fortunate to have known him.

Frankie McWhorter, mounted on Sunday (1992)

Frankie McWhorter

I've always been attracted to people who had a sense of humor. That is one thing that has drawn me to cowboys—their ability to ignore the ugliness and meanness in this life, and to carry on their affairs as though this planet were a nicer place than it probably is.

Over the years, I've found myself seeking out such people, listening to their stories, learning from them, and applying their insights to my own profession, writing.

Frankie McWhorter is just such a man—a cowboy whose pranks and practical jokes have made him something of a legend in Lipscomb County, Texas.

One day Frankie was driving through the pasture and happened upon a dead bull snake. Not one to waste good material, he threw the snake into the back of his pickup and went on with his business.

Later that day, he found himself in front of the house of a cowboy friend. We'll call him Joe. Frankie knew that Joe had been going through some rough times. He and his wife had had a big blowup several weeks before and she had gone to live with relatives. He needed some cheering up. Also, he had pulled a few pranks on Frankie that had never been avenged.

Frankie knocked at the door. When no one answered, he slipped inside and left the dead snake between the sheets of Joe's bed.

What he couldn't have known was that Joe's wife would return home that very evening. She was sorry for whatever part she had played in their troubles. Joe was sorry too. They talked things out, kissed and made up, and for the first time in weeks, they prepared to share the same sleeping quarters.

They turned out the light and crawled between the sheets— and a terrible scream pierced the stillness of night as the lady's foot came to rest upon the cold, coiled snake. The prank turned out to be funnier than Frankie had ever intended, but, alas, he was unable to take credit for it, since it might have cost him his life.

Frankie's circle of friends included a number of cowboys who shared his admiration for an elaborate prank, and would go to great lengths to set one up. Frankie was one of their favorite targets.

Charlie Coffee of the Oasis Ranch and Ronnie Hill of the Canadian River Cattle Company fell into this category. Charlie and Ronnie worked on adjoining ranches in the sand hill country between Higgins and the Canadian River, and they often helped each other in their work.

Another thing they did together was to hunt and trap feral hogs along the Canadian River. A feral hog, in case you don't know, is a domestic animal that has escaped the bonds of civilization and gone back to the wild. Ronnie and Charlie trapped them and used them as a source of groceries.

On this occasion they had finished skinning and quartering a hog when it occurred to them that it would be a shame to waste the hide and head. They drove twenty miles north to the Gray Ranch, whose foreman, Mr. Frankie McWhorter, happened to be gone for the day.

These rascals knew that Frankie had agreed to help one of the neighbors with roundup work the next morning, which meant that he would have to start his day around 4:30 A.M.

Sure enough, the next morning he fell out of bed with his gray hair looking like the mop of a punk rocker. He pulled on his clothes, started the coffee to brewing, stumbled over Clyde the cat at the back step, and headed for the barn. There, with his eyes still pressed into an Oriental shape and barely able to focus, he hit the light switch just inside the barn door, struggled with the hasp on the saddle room door, threw it open, and—looked into the eyes and open mouth of a wild hog.

Charlie and Ronnie had borrowed one of Frankie's saddle racks, which consisted of a thirty-gallon barrel on legs. They had draped the hide over the barrel, propped the head up with a stick, and fixed the mouth so that it stayed open, showing the tusks of the brute in all their hideous glory.

After running backwards for fifty yards and building a new door on the north side of the barn, Frankie had no trouble staying awake.

I'm proud to report that I've pulled a few good ones on Frankie myself. One hot summer afternoon in 1987, we had finished counting the steers in one of his pastures. On the way back to headquarters, we stopped at the grocery store in Higgins.

Frankie pushed his cart around the store and filled it with the items you'd expect a single cowboy to choose—vienna sausage, saltine crackers, vienna sausage with mustard, coffee, and vienna sausage with catsup.

As he wheeled the cart into the checkout station, his gaze fell upon a clear plastic case that contained four nice, plump glazed donuts.

The checkout lady was busy with another customer just then, so Frankie winked at me and said, "Watch this." He lifted the lid, removed one of the donuts, took a huge bite out of it, and put it back.

When the lady began ringing up his purchases, he said, "Oh, and I'll take one of them donuts too." She went to the display case, opened it, and stared at the donut that had been bitten.

She pretended not to see it, but Frankie wasn't about to let her off the hook. "What in the world is going on around here? Are y'all selling *used* donuts now? Why, that's shameful!"

The poor lady blushed and denied any knowledge of it, and by that time she had figured out that she had been a victim of one of Frankie's pranks.

He cackled and told her to ring up the donut on his bill. She started ringing up Frankie's groceries and got another surprise. There, in the cart of this unmarried cowboy, was a box of disposable diapers for a newborn infant!

I had slipped the box into the cart while Frankie was pulling his donut prank. If I hadn't started laughing, the lady would have rung up the diapers and sacked them up, and then spread the word all over Lipscomb County that Frankie McWhorter had a new baby out at the ranch.

About a year later, I drove out to the ranch on a Monday evening to help Frankie ship some big steers early Tuesday morning. At eleven o'clock I said good night and went off to the guest bedroom. This room and a bathroom had been added on to the main house and were separated from the living room by a door.

As I was leaving, Frankie said, "I'll be in the bathroom in a while to take a shower. I'll try not to wake you up."

I grinned, closed the door, and began looking around for "raw materials." I found an upright Hoover vacuum sweeper over in the corner and moved it into the bathroom; dressed it up in a long-sleeved shirt, with one arm resting on the bathtub, and placed a cap over the top of the handle. I positioned it in front of the sink, back just far enough so that the door would open without hitting it. To a sleepy pair of eyes, it would look like a dwarf wearing a baseball cap.

I didn't fall asleep. Lurking beneath the sheet, I watched Frankie enter the room. He had stripped down to his skivvies and was carrying a clean change of drawers. I could see that his mind was a thousand miles away.

He hit the light switch and opened the door. There was a moment of silence, and then the entire house shook as he performed the near-impossible feat of slamming the bathroom door while jumping clear across the room.

It was very impressive.

Somewhere in mid-flight, he got separated from his clean underpants. I'm not sure he ever found them.

One day in the summer of 1989 I was helping Frankie with some cattle work. He was summering some heifers that year and he wanted to ride through them, look them over, and get a good count. It was along towards evening when we jumped our horses out at a two-section place southwest of Higgins. I was riding my mare, Calypso, and Frankie was mounted on a colt.

As usual, Frankie's cowdog went along. His name was Hank, named after some dog in a book. According to Frankie, he was a heck of a fine dog.

We found four heifers that didn't belong in the pasture and tried to drive them to a set of pens. When one of them broke and ran, I gave chase and tried to turn her back to the pens. She didn't turn and I had to rope her.

By the time I got her roped, we were some three hundred yards north of the pens. I got her shut down and gave her a minute to catch her breath, then rode around behind her and tried to drive her back south on a loose rope.

But by then, she had made up her mind to go west, and my efforts to coax her south didn't work. While Calypso and I were going south, the heifer was out at the end of the rope, at right angles to us, fighting to go west.

I tried to drag her through the sand hills, but she was too big for my mare. She was choked down and mad and ready to fight.

Frankie came riding up, accompanied by his cowdog. "Let's see if Hank can change her mind. Bite her, Hank!"

He did, only he bit the wrong end. Instead of biting her on the hind legs, which might have caused her to want to go to the pens, he bit her on the nose, which caused her to want to attack.

Frankie began shouting for him to quit. Hank took this to mean, "Bite her some more on the nose," and he did. All at once Hank was at the center of a storm. The heifer wanted to kill him, and so did Frankie. It was just a question of which one could get to him first.

Frankie lost his temper. He bailed out of the saddle and took after Hank, who suddenly looked bewildered and sorrowful.

I was holding the heifer on a tight rope. Frankie stormed over to Hank and aimed a ferocious kick at his tail-section, but Hank moved and Frankie missed.

His boot went so high in the air that it pulled a muscle in the back of his leg. He squalled in rage and pain, grabbed his thigh with both hands, and began hopping around on one leg.

This spooked the colt, which began running backwards, dragging the crippled Frankie along with him.

At that same moment, the heifer decided to kill Frankie instead of the dog, and she charged right into the middle of him. Frankie grabbed her in a headlock, held tight to the colt's reins, and continued screaming and kicking at his loyal dog.

Frankie's version of the story is that I intentionally fed slack to the heifer. That's not true. I wouldn't have done such a mean thing to a cowboy friend.

The problem was that I was laughing so hard, I almost fell out of the saddle, so it's no wonder that a little slack crept into the rope.

What made it particularly funny was, that very morning, Frankie had given me a progress report on Hank's training—"He's really coming along and makin' a hand."

Frankie, who used to play fiddle with Bob Wills and the Texas Playboys, entertains a crowd of cowpunchers after a spring branding (1998)

Well, he'd *tried* to make a hand. What really impressed me was that while Frankie was wrestling with the heifer, old Hank jumped up and licked him on the ear.

Now boys, that's a heck of a cowdog.

In the spring of 1988, Frankie invited me to ride horseback with him in a parade in Higgins, Texas. I knew it was a bad idea. Ranch horses aren't used to the noise and commotion of a parade, and pavement is hard when you get bucked off on it.

But, since Frankie had been talked into riding in the parade, I figured it might be all right. Frankie was a top hand, and he had offered to let me ride one of his horses. Heck, it might even turn out to be fun.

Frankie gave me the choice of riding Bernie or Flower. Well, that was the easiest decision of the year. I chose Bernie without a moment's thought. He was calm and sensible, Frankie's Number One pasture horse.

But Flower? Well, if a guy was to go shopping for a horse he NEVER wanted to ride in a parade, he'd pick Flower, a paint horse that had been named by somebody with a sense of humor.

Flower was no buttercup. In fact, he had what we might call "a criminal record."

For starters, he'd come out of Bennie Beutler's string of rodeo broncs—a real bad starter as far as I was concerned. A rancher around Arnett, Oklahoma, had given the horse to Frankie just to get him off the place.

Frankie and Flower had been together for several years, and those years had been stormy. I knew that on at least one occasion he had pitched him off in the pasture. Another time, Flower had bucked across the gravel drive in front of the house and ended up wedged between a tree and the yard fence.

Frankie had found himself so mashed that he couldn't spur, pull a rein, or get off, and the two of them sat there until the goat came along and Flower decided to follow him to the barn.

I felt a little guilty, picking Bernie and leaving Frankie to ride

Flower, but these gray hairs in my beard have made it easier for me to live with such guilt.

On the morning of the parade, Frankie saddled Flower and Bernie and brought them into town in his gooseneck trailer. I met him at the high school at 10:30 A.M. I put on my spurs and chinks, and was kind of excited about riding old Bernie in the parade. I just hoped that Flower wouldn't pull any dirty tricks on Frankie.

Frankie had already unloaded Flower and was riding him around the staging area, getting him used to all the strange sights and noises. So far, Frankie hadn't been bucked off. I opened the trailer gates, caught Bernie's rein, and led him out. He *flew* out, and when he hit the ground, his ears were up at the top of the flagpole.

His neck had acquired the shape of a hay hook, he had rollers in his nose, he was dancing on his front feet, and his eyes reminded me of two fried eggs, sunny-side-up.

He dropped his head and pointed a mule-drawn wagon that was clattering past, only a few feet away. It was about then that my mouth went dry.

This couldn't possibly be Bernie's first parade—could it?

Frankie rode up. I was chasing Bernie around in a circle, trying to pull up the cinch a notch or two. Frankie studied the situation. "You know, come to think of it, I guess old Bernie's never been to a parade before."

"Say, that's great news, Frankie."

"But I never dreamed he'd act this way."

I wondered about that. This was the same Frankie McWhorter who would tie your shirt sleeve in a knot, flip a head of grass burrs onto the seat of your pants, take the loop out of your catch rope, pour salt into your coffee, or turn a turtle loose under the seat of your pickup.

I couldn't tell. His face showed as much innocence as you could expect from such a man, but that wasn't comforting.

We rode in the parade. That was the longest mile I ever rode! I never dreamed that the little town of Higgins, population 702, could hold so many boogers. And Bernie saw them all—

Mule wagons outfitted with jingle bells, clanking frying pans, and crepe paper streamers. Green-broke mules walking on their hind legs, ladies in Arabian costumes, with robes flapping in the breeze, and fire trucks with sirens going. Barking dogs, paper cups rolling along the ground, and kids—on lawn mowers, bicycles and four-wheelers. Floats that hissed, growled, flapped, and discharged strange patterns of bubblegum and candy.

As Bernie crow-hopped past the announcer's stand at the center of town, I squeezed up a wooden smile and waved a wet palm towards the crowd. I probably looked about as happy as a man with malaria. I was.

Ace Reid had once warned me about riding in a parade: "Don't do it." I should have listened. Every gentle horse is just a killer in disguise. All he needs is a parade to bring it out.

There was just one thing that puzzled me about all this— Flower. That hardened criminal, that outlaw, that rodeo veteran had SLEEP WALKED through whole parade! I mean, in the midst of sirens, honking horns, braying mules, barking dogs, and noisy kids, that horse hadn't even lifted an ear! How could that be? I asked Frankie about it.

"Oh well, he's deaf, you know. Can't hear a thing."

Andy was a Cowboy

I guess what fascinated me about Andy was that I never understood him. I thought I did. I thought I knew him pretty well. We rode together on the Beaver River back in the 1970s, and he was as good a cowboy as I ever met, maybe the best.

But twenty years later, his story remains a chord that won't resolve. I admired him deeply, and so did every cowboy who rode with him, but we are all left with the feeling that Andy died too young, and that his life just didn't turn out right.

He was probably pushing fifty years old when I knew him. In cowboy-years, that's pretty old. The attrition rate is fierce in that business and it's a rare man who stays with it that long. Those who do, reach their prime between forty-five and fifty. If they're not too crippled-up to work, they become the elite.

That's where Andy was when I rode with him. He was a cowboy in his prime. He could do it all, and he did it without effort.

I used to position myself at roundups so that I could follow him around and study the way he handled horses and cattle. He made everything look so easy—no wasted motion, no false starts, no jerky movements, no mistakes. Even around wild cattle, he seemed to flow like cream.

I doubt that we ever found out just how much he knew about cattle, horses, and roping. No one ever came out and asked him, and he wasn't the kind of man who cared to show off. He had nothing to prove to anybody. When a calf broke from the herd, it was the young bucks like me who went after him and brought him back on the rope. Andy would just slouch in the saddle and watch.

I remember the last day I worked with Andy. It was toward the end of April 1979, and by that time I had already heard the news that he was leaving the Beaver River country. No one knew why, exactly. There was some talk about his wife. She wasn't happy out on the ranch—and she was definitely *out* on a ranch. Where they lived wasn't close to anything. Andy liked it that way but she didn't.

I really hated to see him leave.

We had a late spring that year. The weather stayed cool and damp through the first half of April. Then, around the fifteenth, the weather warmed up and in three days' time, spring exploded upon our valley. Green grass shot up in the meadow pastures, wild plum burst into bloom, and flights of cranes began winging their way north.

On April 26 I got the phone call I had been waiting for. One of the cowboys on the next ranch told me that tomorrow morning, we would begin the spring roundup season. Since Andy and I lived on the same side of the river, we were assigned to jump our horses out at the same spot in the pasture. Andy had to drive past the ranch where I lived, so he would pick me up on the road at daylight.

I made sure I wasn't late. Instead of getting up at 5:00 A.M., as I normally would have, I set the alarm for 4:30 A.M., and at daylight old Star and I were waiting in the road. It was a lovely morning, neither warm nor cold. A fresh breeze out of the south-east carried the smells of sagebrush and new grass, and the sun was lost behind a line of smoky gray gulf clouds.

It had rained an inch and a half in the night, and water was standing in the road. Andy had eight miles of muddy road to pull in his pickup and trailer and he was running late, so I rode Star up the hill to meet him. At last I heard the groan of his pickup and saw the blue four-wheel drive pop over a sand hill. His pickup and trailer were moving like a snake down the road, and the pickup was throwing up mud balls with all four wheels.

He slid to a stop and I loaded Star into the back compartment of the trailer. Up in the front compartment stood old Hammer, Andy's horse for the day. He was a thin-hipped bay who had the ugliest head of any horse in the country. At a certain angle, it bore a striking resemblance to a claw hammer, or the head of a de-horned moose.

I think Andy got a kick out of riding that ugly thing. If any-body else had showed up at a roundup with such a creature, the other cowboys would have written him off as a rookie. Andy could get by with it, because he was Andy.

Poor old Hammer didn't know how ugly he was, and out in the pasture, when he had Andy on his back, it didn't matter. Andy made outrageous claims for the horse, said he could pen a mouse in a three-section pasture, run a prairie dog down his hole and then dig him out with his hooves. The truth was that Hammer was an average horse—carrying an exceptionally good cowboy.

I climbed into the pickup. "Say, that sure is a beautiful horse you've got back there."

Andy laughed. "Yes sir. That head looks like it was whittled out of a bois d'arc post, don't it?"

We headed west down the muddy road, and it was then that I caught the smell of whiskey. That puzzled me. I had worked with Andy for more than a year and I had never smelled liquor on him.

The average citizen who grew up on western movies might suppose that drinking is commonplace among cowboys, but that's far from the truth. In our country, a cowboy never showed up for work with whiskey breath. It just wasn't done.

I watched Andy closer now, looking for changes in his manner that would confirm that he had been drinking. I found them. He talked more than usual, and in a louder voice. I noticed that he slurred a few of his words.

I turned away and stared out the window. I felt betrayed. I could accept that the rest of us had weaknesses, but Andy?

I didn't know it then, but he had a long history of this sort of thing. He had fought the jug most of his life. I had known him during one of his good periods, and now he was going into a slide.

We stopped on a hill in the northeast corner of the pasture we were to round up. Andy gazed down toward the river and said that the other boys were slow getting into position, probably because of the rain. We would just sit a while and wait.

He poured some coffee out of a thermos and started talking.

He told of growing up on a ranch in West Texas, working under a stepfather he didn't like, leaving home and going to work on a ranch in New Mexico.

He said he stayed out with the wagon and had trouble getting along with the boss, an older man who had gotten his grinners (front teeth) knocked out and didn't have much use for young bucks who still had theirs. If they still had their front teeth, they couldn't be very tough.

One morning before daylight, the cowboys were holding the horse herd inside a circle of ropes while the wagon boss roped their mounts for the day. When he came to Andy, he yelled, "Who do you want today?"

"I don't want one."

"What's wrong, you sick?"

"No, I quit."

"No, you don't quit. We've got work to do."

"Without me."

The boss glared at him. "Okay, that's fine. We don't need you anyway. Get off the ranch."

"You'll have to take me back to headquarters." The wagon was thirty miles away from headquarters, and the boss had the only car.

"Sorry, I've got work to do."

"After you take me back."

"Walk. It's only thirty miles. It'll do you some good."

Andy dropped his ropes, stepped into the circle, and walked up to the boss. "You're going to take me back to headquarters or there won't be a cactus bush left in New Mexico, after I finish whipping you with them."

The boss gave him a ride back to headquarters and dumped him out. Carrying his saddle and gear, Andy hitched a ride to Gallup and joined the Marine Corps, "to take a little rest and get away from all the violence," he said with a smirk.

Now Andy glanced out the window again and saw men on horseback moving down the broad meadows along the river. "It's time to go," he said. He stepped out of the pickup, pulled on a battered pair of shotgun chaps, and climbed up on Hammer, poked him hard with his spurs and galloped off into the hills, singing a song.

I never got the chance to tell him goodbye or to thank him for the things he had taught me. The next day he was gone.

There are still big stretches of this country where a man can be alone, where he can walk outside at night and look from horizon to horizon and see only moon and stars up there—no lights, no towns, no houses.

A lot of people consider darkness the enemy. Those who appreciate emptiness and darkness seem backward, old-fashioned, even a little strange, and they often end up working on ranches, miles away from the nearest town.

Maybe they *are* a little strange, and maybe there is something in those towns they're trying to avoid. Andy was turned that way. As long as he stayed out on the ranch, he got along fine. But when he went to town, he found trouble. If he had stayed out with the livestock, he'd probably be alive today. But he didn't, and he's dead.

If you work as a cowboy, you see a lot of men who come and go. Some starve out. Some have trouble with their wives. Some are just born with an itch they can't scratch, and they move on for no particular reason. Most of those guys fade from your memory after a while, but I've never been able to put Andy out of my mind.

It must have been six or eight months later when one of my cowboy friends called and asked, "Have you heard the news about Andy?" I said no.

Andy had moved to town and started hanging out in beer joints. He was drinking again. One day at the feed store, he got into an argument with the proprietor, over a dime.

"Andy did what he always did when he was ready to fight. He cocked his right shoulder back and grinned, then he brought that big right fist around and knocked the man into the back room. Any time old Andy goes to grinning, you want to watch out."

I thought maybe that was the end of the news, but it wasn't. For several months, there had been a rash of thefts in our area. Someone was stealing horses and stock trailers. The sheriff suspected that it was the work of professional thieves, so he called in the Texas and Southwest Cattle Raisers Association inspector to handle the case.

It was interesting, how they traced the horse stealing back to Andy. All the stolen horses were well-bred, high-dollar horses, and several of them had been caught out in the pasture at night. The thief was not only an expert on bloodlines, but to have caught those horses at night, he had to be "much cowboy."

During the investigation, one of the ranchers involved made the off-hand comment, "The only man I know who could have pulled that off is Andy Samson." He said that, never dreaming it might be true. But the TSCRA inspector heard it and didn't forget, and Andy became a victim of his own reputation.

The inspector moved in and started putting the clues together, and they all pointed to Andy, whom the inspector had known and liked for years. He found Andy at the beer joint and asked if he had done it. Andy smiled and said that he had.

He didn't lie. He told the inspector everything he had stolen (and it was no small amount, maybe a dozen stock trailers and as many horses) and exactly how he had done it.

"But I never stole a horse that belonged to a cowboy," Andy told him, "and I never took another man's saddle."

He didn't seem angry or particularly surprised at being caught, and he made no attempt to resist arrest. The inspector took him to jail and booked him for felony theft.

When Jake told me this story, I was speechless. I would have trusted Andy with anything I owned. I couldn't believe that he had become a common criminal.

"It's the drinking," said Jake. "He was a different man when he got on that jug."

Because Andy cooperated with the authorities, and because the TSCRA inspectors held him in such high esteem, they worked behind the scenes to get him a probated sentence. "Andy Samson doesn't belong in the penitentiary," they said, "and Texas doesn't need the expense of keeping him there."

They talked with the judge and worked out the terms of his probation. They would help him find a job and he could start paying back the people he had wronged.

I lost track of Andy for a year or so, but every time I ran into my old cowboy friends, I asked them if they had heard any news. No one had heard anything.

Then, in the summer of 1984, I got some news. Andy was working for a feedlot in west Texas; I decided to give him a call.

I called the feedlot and was told that Andy was out in the yard. I left my number and asked that he call me back.

It was around seven o'clock in the evening when the call came. I was excited, hearing his voice again after five long years, but my excitement soon faded. I could hardly understand what he said, and then it struck me that he was so drunk he could hardly talk.

I ended the conversation as quickly as I could.

Then, a few months later, Jake called again. Andy's story had finally ended and he knew I'd want to know.

"He got deep into the bottle and couldn't get out. He lost his job and his wife left him. They revoked his probation and had him in jail down in Lubbock. One night he had an asthma attack, and before they could get him to a hospital, he died."

"That's a sorry end for a good man," I said.

There was a long silence. Then Jake said, "Andy was a cowboy."

I'll never understand Andy Samson, or why he destroyed the man we all admired so much. I guess he did the best he could. I'm glad I knew him, and I'm sorry I never had a chance to tell him so.

Part Two
COWBOYS

Dave Nicholson, Canadian River cowboy, drags a calf
to the branding fire (1999)

Dave Nicholson and the Pickle Snow Cone

In July 1998 my son Mark and I made our annual trip to the Pampa Rodeo. On our way, we stopped at the C Bar C ranch and picked up our friend and neighbor, Dave Nicholson.

The Pampa Rodeo is a Professional Rodeo Cowboys Association show, with the stock furnished by Beutler and Gaylord of Elk City, Oklahoma. Benny Beutler knows how to put on a rodeo, and you can always count on seeing great bulls, great broncs, and pickup men who are skilled enough to be a show on their own.

Dave had been attending this rodeo for many years and had a certain spot where he always sat, on the east side, right in front of the bucking chutes. After we had eaten at the free barbecue, we took our places in Dave's favorite spot.

Sure enough, it offered a great view of the roughstock events. The only problem was that it was also the hottest place in the whole Panhandle, directly in the blaze of the evening sun and without a whisper of wind.

Maybe that explained why we were the only ones sitting in that section. With sweat rolling down the back of my neck and dripping off the end of my nose, I said to Dave, "Are you sure you don't want to go sit in the barbecue pit? It might be a little warmer."

Dave replied that I should be glad it wasn't winter, because then we'd be freezing.

Just before the rodeo began, we were joined by a couple of cowboy friends from Lipscomb County, Lance Bussard and J. W. Beeson. These guys had been building fence all summer and had built up a resistance to heat stroke, so this was an ideal spot for them.

About halfway through the rodeo, we had dripped enough sweat so that even Dave was thirsty. He pulled some bills out of his pocket and told Mark to go buy snow cones for the three of us. Mark asked us what flavors we wanted, and we said, "Wet."

He returned with a little cardboard tray and four snow cones, three red and one green. He gave me the green one, which I supposed was lime. I pushed the straw to the bottom and took a big sip, expecting the taste of limeade.

It wasn't. My taste buds went into shock. I whirled around and saw that Mark was laughing. "*What is this?*" Then I identified the taste. It was a dill pickle juice snow cone, the first I had ever encountered.

We both got a good laugh. Then it occurred to me that Lance, sitting to my left, hadn't noticed. I handed him the snow cone. "Here, you want a drink? It's pineapple."

"Sure. I love pineapple." He pushed the straw to the bottom and took a big slurp. His eyes bugged out and he choked. "*What is this?*"

We roared with laughter, and then Lance realized that Beeson hadn't noticed. "Here, try this snow cone. It's pineapple."

Beeson was a bit daintier than either of us had been. Instead of slurping, he spooned some of the ice into his mouth. His head swung around to Lance. "It almost tastes like—pickles."

Another good laugh. Then it occurred to Mark that Dave had been so intent on the rodeo, he'd missed our little sideshow, so Mark handed him the snow cone. "Here. We had one extra. It's pineapple."

Without taking his eyes away from the arena, Dave shoveled some ice into his mouth. He took a couple of bites, then stared down at the cup. He didn't say a word, just spit into the cup, handed it back to Mark, and went on watching the show. He was determined not to give us any satisfaction from the prank.

Well, I had to give Mark credit. It was the best prank of the summer, like catching four rats with the same piece of cheese. I don't think it would have worked on women, though. They would have noticed what was going on around them, but four males at a rodeo? I guess you can do anything, short of setting off a bomb, and they'll never notice.

Clarence Herrington and Cowboy Logic

Clarence Herrington was a bachelor cowboy on the Lazy Y ranch and lived on the old Sam Handley place on Wolf Creek, about twenty miles south of Perryton, Texas.

Back in 1979 when I was cowboying for the Ellzey family, I used to drive past his house every day. You know how cowboys are; we notice the important things—the dogs, the grass in the horse pasture, what's in the back of a man's pickup, what's in the sick pen, how many staples are out of the fence.

Well, I began to notice that Clarence *always* had a bunch of clothes hanging on the clothesline behind his house.

That didn't make an impression on me at first, but after months of driving past his place and still seeing clothes hanging on the line, I started wondering about it.

Was it possible that he washed his clothes every day? No. That didn't fit what I knew of Clarence.

Day after day I puzzled over this mystery. Fall came, and then winter. The clothesline remained full, even on days when the temperature was down around zero.

Now, that wasn't right. Nobody, and especially a cowboy, would wash and hang out clothes in the dead of winter.

And then it hit me. Clarence had created a masterpiece of Cowboy Logic, right there in his back yard.

You see, a normal human would wash clothes, hang them out to dry, gather them up in a basket, take them inside, iron them, fold them, and put them away in drawers.

Clarence had found a way of compressing all those steps down to three. He washed them, hung them out on the line, and *left them there until he was ready to wear them.*

He let the wind do his ironing, he didn't need any folding, and he let the clothesline serve as a chest of drawers. Furthermore, all the non-cowboys in the county thought that he was a real demon for cleanliness.

What a brilliant idea! The economy and simplicity of it almost brought tears to my eyes.

A couple of days later I met Clarence on the road. He was driving the Lazy Y's little gray Jeep. Instead of wearing a hat, he had his head wrapped up in a white bandage, with his hair sticking out on top, so that he looked like Woody Woodpecker marching home from the Civil War.

I asked what happened to his head. Well, he'd branded some steers the day before and he sure was sorry now that he hadn't taken the time to do a little welding on the squeeze chute, because one of the chute levers had clubbed him over the head.

"Well, never mind about the blood and stitches," I said. "I have just figured out why your clothesline is always full. Clarence, you have made me proud to be a cowboy!"

He grinned and narrowed his blacked eyes. "Makes you wonder how they can go on selling clothes dryers, don't it?"

Lance Bussard of Lipscomb, Texas, holds a calf at the Heart Ranch branding (1993)

Lance Bussard's
Broken Collarbone

Lance Bussard is a cowboy pal of mine. He and his family operate the Heart Ranch near the booming metropolis of Lipscomb, Texas, and we swap out ranch work. In the spring we help each other gather and brand, and in the fall we throw in together on our shipping roundups.

Several years ago in the fall, I found myself riding at the back of the herd next to Lance. I hadn't seen him all summer and asked how he'd been. He gave me an odd smile and said, "Well, I had kind of a rough summer. I guess you haven't heard."

No, I hadn't heard. I asked him to tell me about it.

One day in the summer, he was out riding pastures on a horse he had recently acquired and didn't know very well. Something happened all at once. He didn't know whether the horse bucked with him or fell down, but he woke up on the ground, out in the middle of the pasture.

The horse was gone.

Lance had a headache and a biting pain in his shoulder. One

of his arms hung lower than the other one, and it didn't take him long to figure out that he had broken his collarbone.

He got up and started walking. He was in pain and three miles from the house. Several times he thought he might faint, but he rested a while and kept walking. At last he made it to the house and someone drove him into town to see a doctor.

Yep, he had a broken collarbone, and there wasn't much medical science could do about it. The doc gave him a shoulder harness, told him to take it easy, stay off of horses and away from posthole diggers, and let the bones heal.

When the pain bothered him, he could take aspirin. Oh, and soaking in a tub of hot water might speed up the healing.

"That was the only good part about the whole deal," said Lance. "All at once I had an excuse for spending time in my new hot tub, instead of digging postholes in the sun."

He soon learned that for an adult male cowboy, a broken collarbone was no laughing matter. The pain was constant and severe, and there wasn't much he could do on the ranch, so he lay around and spent a lot of hours in his new hot tub. That thing came in mighty handy.

The weeks passed and he could feel the bones healing up. The pain began to ease, but he didn't try to push it. He sure didn't want to mess things up and go through it all over again. One broken collarbone per summer was about enough for him.

He took it easy, stayed off of broncs and fencing crews, and put a lot of miles on that hot tub. The collarbone got better every day, until at last he decided he was whole again. Tomorrow, he would go back to work, a new man.

But just to be sure, he would take one last treatment in the hot tub. He stripped off his clothes and went into the bathroom. He knelt on the edge of the tub and leaned over to turn on the hot water.

His dog was inside the house. This was no ordinary ranch mutt. He was the kind of loyal dog who *really cared* about his master and would do anything to help. Seeing his master naked and stretched out on the edge of the hot tub, he rushed into the bathroom to lend a hand.

He cold-nosed Lance in a sensitive spot.

Lance's mind was a thousand miles away. He didn't know the dog was anywhere around. That cold nose shocked him so badly that he let out a scream and flew into the hot tub.

Unfortunately, it hadn't filled up with water and he broke his collarbone again, in the same place.

"I sure wanted to kill that dog," said Lance, "but he ran, and I was hurting so bad I couldn't catch him."

By the time he finished the story, I had begun to worry about my own collarbones. I was laughing so hard, I feared I might fall off my mare.

Marshall Cator

I met Marshall Cator for the first time in 1984. Dave Nicholson, Mr. Cator's foreman on the Lips ranch, had invited me to his winter branding in December. I accepted. Even though I had an aversion to working cattle in bitter cold, I wanted to attend the branding because I knew that Mr. Cator would be there and I would get a chance to meet him.

I had heard about him, of course. In the northern Texas Panhandle, Marshall Cator was a living legend. I'll bet there wasn't a cowboy in the whole area who didn't know his name. You could walk into any saddle shop in the Panhandle, any boot shop or feed store, any livestock auction, any roping or rodeo, and hear a story about Marshall Cator.

What you heard was that he was one generation removed from the Cator brothers of Hansford County, Englishmen who were among the first settlers in the Panhandle, along with Thomas Bugbee, Charles Goodnight, and A. J. Springer. They hunted buffalo in the late 1870s and operated out of a stockade called Zulu.

Young Marshall began running his own cattle at an early age and he followed the cow over the course of his long life, buying and leasing ranches from the Canadian River on the south to the Cimarron on the north. I've heard it said that at one time, he was the largest individual owner of mother cows in the state of Texas.

What is most astounding about the many stories I have heard about Marshall Cator is that none has ever been critical. Men who have known and worked beside him for decades speak his name with reverence.

Jim Streeter, my neighbor down on the river, was one of them. He started working for Mr. Cator as a young man, on a ranch on the Cimarron River, and later followed him down to the Lips Ranch on the Canadian. He probably knew Marshall Cator as well as any man alive. They rode together in the prime of their lives and grew old together.

Jim was a plain-spoken man and a harsh judge of human character, but when he spoke of his old friend, his eyes softened and a smile came to his face.

"I'll tell you one thing about Marshall Cator. Whichever part of the job was hardest, toughest, dirtiest, or most dangerous, Marshall did it. He never asked his men to do anything that he wouldn't do himself. He was the first man there in the morning and the last to leave at night."

Dave Nicholson added his own brief superlative: "Marshall Cator is a cowman."

And what is a *cowman*? He is a man with a deep understanding of cattle, horses, and cowboys, and the ranch land they share. He brings unity and purpose to the operation and leaves them all better than they were before.

The stories about Mr. Cator tell of a man who was honest in his dealings and respectful of his employees; who knew cattle the way Webster knew the English language; an expert horseman, a deadly roper, and a tireless worker.

I made Dave promise on his Solemn Cowboy Oath to introduce us at the fall branding.

He did. It came during a lull in the branding work. Mr. Cator, a tall gaunt man in his mid-eighties, stepped off his horse and warmed his hands at the branding fire. Dave saw his chance.

"Marshall, this is John Erickson. He's a writer and he wanted to meet you."

Mr. Cator held me in his gaze, ungloved his right hand and shook mine. "Oh yes. I've read your articles."

"I've sure heard a lot about you."

"Oh?"

"Yes sir. You're sort of a legend, it seems."

"Huh."

And that was it. He went back to dragging calves and didn't say another word to me the rest of the day. I thought maybe I had offended him or that he didn't like writers. But Dave said no, that was just Marshall. He may have been a living legend, but he was so shy and modest that he hardly ever talked, even to his close friends.

In 1994 Mr. Cator gave up his lease on the ninety-four-section Lips ranch and sold his herd of Hereford cows to the Courson family of Perryton.

He decided it was time to cut down on his workload. He was beginning to slow down with age and his eyesight wasn't so good. Spending twelve hours a day in the saddle wore him out more than it used to. He was ninety-two-years old.

After the Courson family bought Mr. Cator's cow herd on the Lips Ranch, they invited him to come back and help gather one of the pastures. This was one of those big pastures of fifteen sections or so. The men trailered their horses to the north end, met on the flats before daylight, and drove the cattle off the caprock to pens near the river.

At the end of the day, Mr. Cator and his horse were quite a distance from the pickup and trailer that would take them back home to Sunray, an hour-and-a-half drive. Harold Courson noted that it was getting dark and offered to drive Mr. Cator to his pickup.

"Oh, I'll just ride, thanks. It's only seven miles."

Riding seven miles through rugged canyons, in the dark and after a hard day's work, was no big deal to Marshall Cator. He'd been doing it most of his ninety-two-years. The only difference was that now he was almost blind.

The next time I worked cattle with him was in the spring of 1995, when I went over to the Lips ranch to help Dave with his spring branding. We were gathering a pasture of some fifteen sections. Dave took most of the twenty-one cowboys to the north end of the pasture. He left me and a few others to clear out the timber and tamarack brush along the river. He told me that Marshall would be working the river just east of me.

He was ninety-three-years old and his eyesight was so bad that he had been forced to stop driving. I asked Dave, "If his eyes are so bad that he can't drive, how's he going to get along horseback in a 9,000 acre pasture?"

Dave shrugged. "I don't know, but he does."

I was curious about this, and later that morning I had a chance to observe him at close range. My son Mark and I had ridden out our section of the river bottom. We had located some cows and calves in the tamarack brush and were sitting on our horses, waiting for the crew up north to come out of the hills with their cattle.

I heard the snap of brush to the east and saw a man on a bay horse riding towards us in an easy trot. It was Marshall Cator. We were straight in front of him and in plain sight, but I soon realized that Mr. Cator couldn't see us. He had ridden out his section of the river and had strayed into ours.

Just then Mark, who was twelve, whispered, "Dad, someone's coming." Instantly, Mr. Cator's horse did a ninety-degree turn and began moving north. He had heard Mark's voice. Then some cattle moved, causing the brush to snap. Mr. Cator altered course and headed straight for them.

So that was how he did it. Without good eyes to guide him, he was going strictly on sound, and perhaps taking cues from his horse's ears.

Later, when we had penned the herd, Mr. Cator took his turn roping and dragging calves to the branding fire. He missed a few loops, which wouldn't have happened in his prime, but he roped as well as I and some of the other cowboys did.

That afternoon, as Mark and I loaded our horses in the stock trailer, I said, "Mark, I want you to remember this day. You saw a man ninety-three-years old roping calves."

It's important that our kids know and remember that men like Marshall Cator have walked this earth.

(L to R): Laura Streeter, Mark Erickson, and Jim Streeter (1993)

Jim Streeter

I met Jim Streeter in the spring of 1972. I was doing research for a book about the Canadian River valley in the Texas Panhandle, and Jim was a man I simply had to interview. He'd cowboyed on the river for twenty years and knew its stories and characters as well as any man alive.

Jim was the foreman on the 17,000-acre Tandy ranch. He and his wife Laura lived in the old Tandy house on the river, and since they didn't have a telephone, I had a hard time making an appointment to meet him. Finally, I stopped writing him letters and just drove down to the place, and found him working on a windmill in a pasture above the caprock.

There, we shook hands and I tried to explain my writing project. Jim listened without much comment. His manner seemed gruff at first, but beneath his stern exterior lurked a keen mind and a lively sense of humor. Jim was a man who had mastered his little piece of the world and knew it to the bone— the land, the animals, the work, and the people—and I soon understood why he was so highly respected by everyone who knew him.

Even though I was accustomed to the dry wit of the cowboy tribe, Jim's humor often caught me off guard. He rarely announced his witticisms with a smile, but delivered them almost carelessly. Sometimes it took me hours or days to figure out who or what had been skewered on the forks of his satire.

One of my favorite Jim Streeter stories concerned a horse of mine. Dollarbill had an annoying habit of rolling in the dirt while the saddle was still on his back, and one day I said, "Mr. Streeter, what do you do about a horse that rolls with the saddle on?" He gave me a blank stare and said, "Take it off."

I had expected some arcane horse training technique. He had given me common sense.

In June 1972, photographer Bill Ellzey and I made a 150 horseback trip down the Canadian River valley, tying together my year of research for the book. We ended up spending two nights with Jim Streeter on the Tandy ranch, and I had the opportunity to spend hours taking down his stories and observations. When the book came out in 1978, Jim Streeter was its most important character and contributor.

I had long dreamed of owning a piece of that magnificent Canadian River valley, and in 1990 I got my chance when the nine-section Hodges ranch came up for sale. The Hodges place joined the Tandy ranch on the west, so Kris and I became the nearest neighbors (seven miles away) of Jim and Laura Streeter. All three of our children had the opportunity to know the Streeters, and I'm sure they will never forget them.

Jim died in September 1999, after a long struggle against the miseries and indignities of old age. Laura asked me to speak at his funeral, which I considered a high honor. On a windy, cold, miserable morning in September, I read the following poem to a big crowd of Jim's friends, family, and admirers, with Jim's well-used saddle sitting in front of me.

September 28, 1999

I didn't sleep real well last night and woke up many times.
I heard words and meters in my dreams; my head was full of rhymes.
See, Laura called us on the phone and told us yesterday,
And asked if I would care to say a word or two today.

She said, "be brief." I guess she knew there'd surely be a line
Of friends and your admirers who'd want to spend some time
To tell you thanks and adios and speak of their concern.
Every cowboy in this country has an A. J. Streeter yarn.

So I'll be brief, or try to be. It'll put me to the test
To cull the swirling herd of words and cut out just the best
That capture pleasant memories and warm us with their glow,
That take the measure of our friend before we let him go.

When Kris and I first bought that place that joined you on the west,
I was thrilled to be your neighbor and felt very much blessed.
I had but one concern. You see, we had this teenage son.
Old Scot was walking trouble, just like a loaded gun.

I took the boy aside one day; we had a little chat.
I said, "Scot, I know the day will come when you're driving off the cap
And passing through the Tandy ranch and see a bunch of quail.
Temptation's going to tell you that they'd fit your dinner pail.

But listen, sonny boy, 'cause what you might not know
Is there's an old man on the river, drives a red Ford pickup, slow,
And he parks on Tandy Mesa and there he counts his quail.
If he comes up short by just one bird, you'll meet the county jail.

But if you can't resist and you take that skillet shot,
When Jim pulls up for a little talk, I would advise you not

To tell the man a falsehood. He's got radar in those eyes,
and one thing he won't forgive is a man who tells him lies."

And then I said, "Oh, by the way, I think you ought to hear
That I admire old Jim a lot. I've known him many years
And when you look around this world for models of a man,
Remember A. J. Streeter. There's no better in the land."

Well, Jim, we had a norther blow through here the other night.
This valley has the feel of fall, the air a pleasant bite.
We'll be shipping calves tomorrow, and every cowboy on that crew
Will have a smile upon his lips and a memory of you.

But dang it, Jim, you left too soon and now this neighborhood
Is in the hands of me and Brent and Jack. We always understood
You wouldn't be around forever, but don't you think we're awfully green
To be in charge of your old country, without you here on the scene?

And what of Old Man Whitsell's place? Who knows it as you did?
Heck, those cowboys, Dave and Billy D, are hardly more than kids.
And Charlie Coffee, east of town, he's just an ornery pup.
You worked him on the Tandy ranch when he was growing up.

On second thought, the years slip by. We're not such fresh young fellows.
Charlie's losing hair on top and Jack's begun to mellow.
Do you suppose we're old enough to handle this without you?
I reckon we'll find out, and Jim—we'll sure be thinking 'bout you.

Merle Kraft's Roundup

Yesterday around the branding fire, with the north wind howling and the corral dust swirling, I overheard a cowboy say, "Old Merle sure picks pretty days to brand cattle, don't he?"

That drew a laugh from the men standing close enough to hear over the scream of the wind. It was a classic piece of cowboy understatement. The weather was miserable, and so were we.

There were nine of us in the branding pen north of Wolf Creek in Lipscomb County, Texas—ranchers, cowboys, neighbors, and friends of Merle Kraft, whose calves we were branding. It was a Tuesday, around the middle of March.

We all had fading memories of the previous day—sunny, bright, clear, still, warm, the air heavy with the fragrance of spring. It would have been a perfect day to brand cattle and to be horseback with our comrades.

But then around 4:00 A.M. the norther had arrived, bringing overcast skies and winds gusting up to forty-five miles an hour. When my alarm clock went off at 5:00 A.M., I heard the wind rattling the windows and felt a powerful gravitational force to stay in my warm bed. But duty called. I pulled on my warm clothes, saddled and loaded my mare in the trailer, and drove the forty-five miles to Lipscomb.

Around sunup, we hoisted ourselves into cold saddles, pulled our hats down tight to keep them from blowing off, and rode out to gather the cattle.

High wind has a bad effect on cowboys. It causes them to grumble and mutter and cast hard glances at the person responsible for this. (Merle got all the blame for the norther.) Wind also has an unsettling effect on livestock. Even though we had an excellent crew of men, all well-mounted and experienced, we had a hard time gathering the cattle.

In the third pasture, I saw something I'd never seen before. We gathered the pasture from the outside—that is, we pushed all the stock to the center and held them until all the riders came in. The cattle were restless and wanted to run, but we held them in a bunch until they settled down. Then we started the drive west towards the corrals.

We were traveling through sandhills. Lance Bussard and I rode out front in the point position, pinching the lead cows to keep them from running. All went well for ten minutes. It appeared that we had gentled them down.

We topped a sandhill and started down the other side, and that's when the wreck began. All at once, instead of having cows in the lead, we saw a dozen black calves out in front of their mommas. They started running down the hill. Lance and I loped out to hold them back, but they paid no attention to our horses.

Soon they were running at full speed and Lance and I were flying over the sandhills and skunkbrush, trying to turn them back into the herd. They wouldn't turn. They were out of control. Up ahead, I saw a barbed wire fence. I slowed my mare and thought, "When they come to the fence they'll stop and we'll regroup the herd."

They didn't even slow down for the fence. Three of them hit it at full speed and went into the next pasture, while behind me three more calves broke and ran north. This had turned into a full-scale jailbreak, with calves running in all directions. They were running from nothing, running to nowhere, just running.

I galloped north after the three that had cut behind me. When I caught up with them and tried to turn them back south, they split like birds, each going a different direction. It took us an hour and a half to restore order, and those calves never did return to the herd on their own. Those we found had to be roped and tied down, to be picked up later in a stock trailer.

When I got back to the herd, I rode over to Frankie McWhorter, a man rich in knowledge of bovine psychology, and said, "I've never seen calves stampede from their mothers like that. Have you?"

He shook his head. "It was this wind. If we'd gathered them yesterday, they never would have done that."

Heeling calves in such a wind was a humbling experience. The second or third time your loop wraps around your own neck, you begin to think you're not the hotshot roper you thought you were.

We finished the branding around 1:30 P.M. and stopped for lunch. The Lipscomb Cafe had never seen so many dirty faces or so many neon-red eyes as we presented when we tramped in. It had been a hard morning's work, and Merle will hear about it for years to come.

But you know what? We'll all be back next year, even if Merle picks a day that's much worse.

Part Three
CATTLE

The Phantom Cow

There wasn't much about her that stood out in your memory. She was a big red crossbred cow with two stubby horns. She wasn't particularly handsome or ugly, neither fat nor thin. She was just another cow in a herd of cows—until spring roundup in 1994.

On that occasion, we had gathered and penned the Mesa Pasture cattle and were separating the cows and calves. The red cow had some kind of problem with this. First she tried to eat several cowboys. When that failed, she dismantled the northwest corner of the corral fence and headed north towards Picket Canyon.

Greg Hale and I ran for our horses, while other members of the crew made Emergency Sharecropper Repairs on what was left of the fence. The cow had made a mess of it—bent the top steel rod into the shape of her abdomen and changed the angle of the steel corner post.

By the time we got ahorseback, the cow had a three or four minute head start. We galloped north, thinking we would find her near the Picket Canyon fence. It was a pretty good five-wire fence that would stop most cows.

It didn't stop this old rip, and it didn't even slow her down. She jumped it. We followed her tracks to the point where she had cleared the fence. She had gone north, up into the canyon. We rode through the gate and headed north, building loops in our ropes, for it was clear by this time that the red cow had no intention of going back where she belonged.

But if we hoped to get her caught, it would have to be soon. Picket Canyon was a rugged place with big rocks, deep ravines, and dense cedar forests. The farther north you went, the rougher it got and the less inclined you were to pitch a loop on something big and nasty.

We followed her tracks almost a mile into the canyon, and there the trail just disappeared. If we'd had time, we might have been able to pick up the trail, but we didn't. It was obvious that she was a schooled outlaw and that she wanted to be in Picket Canyon more than we wanted her out.

Over the next year or so, I caught sight of her in three different pastures. The sightings were always brief and in the evenings when she came out for water. And she was always alone, an unusual trait to find in a herd animal.

She had come off a ranch near Cimarron, New Mexico, and she felt right at home in our roughest country. Three hundred foot canyon walls that would stop a normal cow didn't cause her any problems. She went where she wished, following trails gouged in the rock by sure-footed mule deer.

I didn't see her the following winter. I thought maybe she had died. But then one day in the spring of 1995 I caught sight of something red up in an isolated ravine in the east pasture. I stopped the pickup and studied the object through field glasses. It was the red cow, and that's when I began calling her the Phantom Cow.

Well, she was still alive, and she even had a calf at her side. That was something of a miracle, since cows that stay off to themselves have trouble making babies. Perhaps she had gotten lost one night and had wandered into the path of an amorous bull.

With spring branding coming up, I wondered if we would ever get her found, gathered, and penned with the other cattle.

When we gathered the pasture, she just happened to be out of the deep canyons, and she happened to be slowed by a calf that wasn't as wild or cunning as she. For that one day at least, her mothering instincts overpowered her urge for solitude.

She got caught in the roundup, but on the two-mile drive to the pens, she was out front every step of the way. Lane Hill and I rode in the point position in front of the herd, and I never took my eyes off of her. At a glance, I could see that she didn't accept our authority and hadn't given up the thought of making a run for the canyons.

But this time we won. We got her inside a new set of pipe corrals that she couldn't jump or tear down, and we even got an M Cross brand on her calf.

After the branding, we drove the herd up a steep winding road that led out of Picket Canyon. Normal cows walked up that hill, and most had to be coaxed along by mounted cowboys who rode along behind. The Phantom Cow *sprinted* up the hill, and by the time we reached the top of the caprock with the rest of the herd, she and her calf had vanished into the wilds of Dykema Canyon or Point Creek Canyon.

We didn't see her for the rest of the summer. By the time I assembled the cowboy crew for the shipping roundup in October, the Phantom Cow was a marked woman. The cowboys knew her and several of them had taken it as a personal challenge to get her gathered.

It happened that she was sighted by two of the most skilled cowboys on the crew—Lane Hill and Frankie McWhorter. Both were well-mounted, would drop a loop on anything with hair, and knew how to handle wild cattle. It was bad luck for the Phantom Cow that she encountered those two Lipscomb County cowboys in open country near the mouth of Point Creek Canyon.

They tried to throw her into the drive, but she turned and attacked their horses. Out came the ropes and she was soon lying on the ground, tied down with Lane Hill's pigging string.

When we had penned the herd, Lane rode over to me. He was wearing a big smile. "We found your Phantom Cow and she's tied down on the east side of the pasture. Shall we take a trailer over there and load her up?"

I said yes. I had decided to sell the old hussy and get her off the place. I asked Lane to describe where they had left her. When he did, it was my turn to smile. "Lane, there's only one road into that canyon. We got a hard rain last week and the road washed out. You couldn't get in there with anything but a bulldozer. You'd better just turn her loose. Maybe you'll get another chance next spring."

And so the Phantom Cow returned to the wild. I looked for her over the winter, when I was feeding the cattle, but I never saw her again. When we gathered the pasture in May 1996, Lane and Frankie were looking for her, but she wasn't there. I was sure by that time that she had finally died, an unrepentant outlaw to the end.

I'm writing this in August 1996. Last evening, Mark and I were driving through the east pasture. On the flats above Dykema Canyon, we saw a cow off to herself. "Now what's wrong with her?" I wondered, driving towards her.

As we drew closer, Mark studied the cow. "Is she one of ours? I don't recognize her."

Neither did I. She was a red crossbred cow with short stubby—"Oh my gosh, Mark, that's the Phantom Cow!" Four months ago she had vanished, and here she was again.

She showed no fear of us and didn't run. She just stared at us, as if to say, "Take a good look, boys, 'cause you might not get another chance."

I called Frankie as soon as I got back to the house and told him the news. He said, "Son, if I was you, I think I'd just leave her alone and let her stay there until she dies. I kind of admire her, don't you?"

He spoke my mind exactly. I wouldn't want a hundred cows like her, but I think we've got room for one Phantom Cow on the M Cross ranch.

Lucky, the Orphan Calf

On this ranch we participate in the rhythms of nature. We experience the seasons through the ebb and flow of water and grass. We witness the birth of animals and we sometimes have to watch them die.

And sometimes we participate in birth and death through the same event.

One Sunday afternoon Mark and I drove over to the far west pasture to check on a stock tank that had been leaking. On our way back to the house, we caught sight of a cow whose posture didn't look just right. She looked uncomfortable, unnatural.

We were calving out some heifers in that pasture and our eyes were trained to pick up such details, which often reveal calving problems. We stopped, backed up, and took a closer look. Sure enough, she seemed to be having trouble delivering her calf.

We gave her an hour to finish the job without our intrusion, but she didn't get it done. We gathered up our calf-pulling equipment and drove the cow to the shipping pens. By this time the sun was dropping in the west and a chill had crept into the north wind.

We snubbed her up to the corral fence and I told Mark that he could handle the delivery. He had assisted me on others, and it was time for him to do one by himself. The calf's front feet and head were in the right place, so I didn't think it would be difficult.

He looped the ends of the O.B. chain around the calf's front hocks, put the calf-puller in place, and began cranking on the ratcheting device that provides the pressure for pulling the calf out of the birth canal.

He cranked and cranked. The calf's front feet and head emerged but its shoulders didn't pop free. The cow groaned and fell to the ground. This was *not* going to be an easy delivery. The calf was too big for the cow's anatomy.

Mark cranked some more. At last the shoulders popped loose and we had the calf halfway out. Mark took up slack and started cranking again. This time, the calf's hips hung up. I got down on the ground with Mark and we both put all our strength into the lever.

We were putting a terrible amount of pressure on the poor calf, enough to pull his joints apart, but I figured he was dead anyway. Our main concern was saving the cow. We had to get the calf out, and we were beyond the point of hauling her to the vet in town. She was down and couldn't stand up, much less load into a stock trailer.

It was almost dark. There was a bite in the wind, yet Mark and I had shed our coats and were sweating. This had turned into a grisly job but we had to finish it.

My wife held the head rope while Mark and I strained and pulled on the cranking device. The calf's hips would not pass through the canal. Out of breath, I stopped to rest. "This is a heck of a way to start your career as a cow gynecologist," I croaked. "I'm not sure we're going to get this done."

Mark kept working. Suddenly the hips popped free and the calf slid out on the ground. And wonder of wonders, he was still alive. So was the cow, even though she had gone through some terrible stress.

I congratulated Mark. On his first solo (sort of) O.B. job, he had saved both mother and child. We left them alone, so that Momma could take care of her business in private. We would check them first thing in the morning.

The next morning Mark left for school before daylight and I checked on the cow and her newly delivered calf. What I saw didn't look good.

Both cow and calf were alive, but neither had moved in the night. I had hoped that after resting up from her ordeal, the cow would get up, lick the calf dry, and get him started nursing. I had hoped for too much.

The stress and pressure we had been forced to use in the delivery had left the cow so crippled she couldn't even raise her head. If anything, the calf appeared to be in even worse shape. His head, mouth, and tongue were swollen from the ordeal. His eyes were rolled back in his head and he was shivering in the cold.

Our celebration of the previous evening had been premature. We thought we had saved both mother and child, but now it appeared that both were slipping towards death.

I found a plastic nipple bottle in the barn, a leftover from the days when our kids raised bottle calves, and returned to the corral. I knew it was important that a calf receives the mother's first milk—colostrum—which contains antibodies that protect the calf from diseases.

I managed to squeeze maybe half a cup of milk from the cow's bag, put the nipple on the bottle, and tried to get the calf to suck. This was a big strapping bull calf, but he couldn't suck. He couldn't even hold his head up. He seemed to be having convulsions, and it occurred to me that we had damaged his nerves, perhaps even his brain, in the process of pulling him out of his mother's body.

I removed the nipple from the bottle, and holding the calf's head off the ground, I poured some of the milk into his mouth. He gasped and gurgled, but he swallowed some of it. I gave him the rest of it. Some of it ended up on the ground, but some of it didn't, and I noticed an immediate change.

He still couldn't stand or lift his head, but he uttered a bleat and seemed stronger.

I dried him off and covered him with a blanket and left. When I returned hours later, the cow seemed closer to death, but the calf was sitting up. I knew by then that the mother was doomed. Her body was damaged beyond repair and she was slipping away. I squeezed out the last of her colostrum milk, not much, and poured it down the calf.

Would he make it? My best guess was that he might survive a few days. His eyes were rolled back in his head. It appeared to me that he had nerve damage and would never be able to function.

But one hopes. I drove into town that afternoon and invested seventeen dollars in a bag of powdered milk-replacer. I was pretty sure that it would turn out to be a bad investment.

That evening, the cow was dead. As far as I could determine, she had never even raised her head. But the calf was looking a little better and stronger. He was trying to stand up and walk. I got some of the store-bought milk down him and moved him to another location, where he would have some shelter from the elements. Twice a day, I continued to pour milk into his mouth, and some of it made it into his stomach.

The little guy had the will to live, he had some fight, but would that be enough? I had to be honest. I didn't think so. He was still spastic. He couldn't stand or walk, and he still didn't have the coordination to suck the bottle.

A calf that can't suck doesn't have much of a future in this world. But as long as the little feller was willing to try, we wouldn't give up either.

Three days after his traumatic arrival in the world, our orphan calf was gaining strength. He was able to stand and even walk a few steps, but the prognosis still didn't look good.

He still showed signs of nerve damage, perhaps permanent. In the first place, he couldn't walk in the normal manner. He couldn't stand on his front hooves, but walked on his knees, with the hooves curled back.

In the second place, his coordination was all messed up. A normal calf is able to start nursing only minutes after he is delivered. Nursing calves seem to have an instinct for doing three things at the same time—they suck, they butt the mother's bag with their heads, and they swish their tails while they're nursing.

Well, our little orphan was three days old and he was so spastic, confused, and messed up, he couldn't get those three operations coordinated. It was pathetic but also a little comical. He seemed to be trying to butt with his tail, wag his tongue, and nurse with his nose.

Kris, Mark, and I continued to feed him bottle milk twice a day, and he continued to get some of it down, but I still wouldn't have bet a nickel that he would survive—although I had already bet a seventeen dollar bag of powdered milk on him.

However, on the fourth day he was walking with one foot down and the other foot curled back, and the next day he was walking on both front hooves. And one morning when I put the nipple in his mouth, he took hold of it and went to sucking.

The next day, everything seemed to fall into place for him. He sucked with his mouth, wagged with his tail, and butted his surrogate mothers with his nose. This was encouraging, and for the first time since the night of his birth, I began to think that the little rascal might actually survive.

Every day he grew stronger. He was turning into a fine, healthy bull calf, with none of the gut problems that often plague bottle calves. When he heard us coming down to the barn, he would jump up and meet us at the gate. If we were late with the grub, he would bawl loud enough so that we could hear him up at the house.

As I write this, he is three weeks old, and I'll swear, there isn't a better, more handsome calf on the ranch. Even though Mark and I almost pulled him in half getting him out, he doesn't show any signs of permanent damage to his feet or nerves.

The main problem we have with him now is that he has too much life and vigor. Once he figured out how to coordinate all those activities—suck, butt, and wag—he became a hazard to our health. After he had butted me twice in a sensitive spot, I began delivering his bottle through a steel gate, with him on one side and me on the other.

But as they say, that's a pretty good problem to have.

Since he's so determined to live, I guess we'll have to give him a name. How about "Lucky?" It fits. The little guy sure beat the odds.

The Floating Cow

One day in September of '95 Mark and I were prowling the east pasture. "Prowling" is a cowboy term for riding the pasture ahorseback. You poke around and look for things you might not see from the pickup.

We were on the south end of the pasture, in a rough area that was hard to reach in a vehicle. Previous owners of the ranch had built a dam there, across a draw that drained Dykema Canyon to the west and several smaller, unnamed canyons to the south.

We'd had some big rains in June and the dam had caught enough water to form a pond of about two acres. Thirty or forty head of cattle were grazing the canyons and watering at the pond, so we rode through the area to check things out.

We found a big red cow lying in the shade of some mesquite bushes. She was off to herself, usually a bad sign. We discovered that she was crippled in one of her back legs. She could get up and hobble to the pond for water, but I knew she couldn't travel well enough to graze and keep herself fed.

Ordinarily, what you do in this situation is rope the cow, drag her into a stock trailer, and take her to a set of pens, where you can keep her fed and watered. But this area was so rough that we couldn't get in and out with a trailer. The only access was a steep trail that came off the caprock. We could get in and out with a four-wheel drive pickup, but pulling a trailer up that washed-out caliche trail was out of the question.

So we started hauling feed to the cow. As long as she had feed and could drink from the pond, she had a chance of surviving.

This worked for several days. Then one evening we found that she had walked into the pond and had gotten into water so deep that she couldn't get out. She had grown weak from struggling and thrashing, and she had even drawn a crowd of buzzards overhead. If we didn't get her out, she would drown.

With some difficulty, we managed to back the pickup down to the edge of the pond. We waded out into the water, put a catch rope around her front feet, tied the other end to the hitch ball on the pickup, and dragged her out on dry land.

Working with her in close quarters, I was able to find the source of her lameness. She had broken her left thigh bone, just below the hip. I knew then that she wouldn't survive and that those buzzards were right. Large animals don't recover from broken bones above the knee.

We left her there with some feed and hoped she would stay out of the water. She didn't, and the next morning we found her dead in the pond. My first thought was that she had gone back into the pond for a drink, which would rank as fairly dumb behavior. But a friend of mine who is a doctor offered another explanation.

"She wanted to stay in deep water because it took the weight off her broken leg." That was an interesting observation, and it might have been correct, but she was just as dead one way as the other. And she had left us with a problem.

We had to pull her out of the pond before she fouled the water, but she had died in a spot we couldn't reach in the pickup. Dragging a 1200 pound cow up a steep bank with nothing but ropes and manpower was out of the question, and we didn't have horses with us.

Then it occurred to me that she was *floating* in water about five feet deep. Gasses inside her body had made her lighter than the water. Was it possible . . .?

My friend Don Weidemann was visiting from Austin. He was a good sport. He and I stripped off our clothes, swam out into the water, and gave the cow a push. Sure enough, she floated away from the shore.

We then proceeded to do something that, to my knowledge, had never been attempted by any crazy cowboy or group of crazy cowboys in Texas history. We swam a dead 1200 pound cow across a pond that was seventy yards across and twenty-five feet deep, using her hulking body as our life preserver.

Like tug boats nudging the Queen Mary, we pushed her to the opposite shore, where my kids and several amazed hunting friends were waiting with the pickup and a chain. We hauled her off. The pond was saved for swimming and stock water.

I lost a good cow but got a great story, and if you happen to be an author as well as a rancher, that's not a bad trade. All cows die, but this story will be told around winter fires for a long, long time.

Geraldine Calf

It was January 1997 and the weather report on Amarillo radio was ominous. Three or four Arctic cold fronts were stacked up and moving our way, and they promised to bring us two weeks of bitter cold weather.

I spent the day preparing. I wrapped the pipes at the bunkhouse (they froze anyway) and gave the cattle extra feed. That morning, on the feed ground in the East Pasture, I noticed an old cow with enlarged teats. She had a small calf following her and I watched them. The calf tried to nurse but couldn't get its mouth around the teats.

Later, I gathered the pair and hauled them to our working pens. I ran the old cow into the chute and milked her out, figuring that now the calf could nurse. With the storm approaching, he would need the milk to survive.

I turned them out into the Mesa pasture, just as the wind shifted to the north and the cold air began moving in. The next morning was frigid, and it was snowing. Around daylight, I drove past the corrals and saw the calf shivering in the cold. He was alone and Momma was nowhere in sight. Several hours later, I located her in Hidden Valley. She wasn't worried about her calf.

What we had here was not just a mechanical problem, but rather a case of child abandonment. Under normal conditions, a cow knows a good deal more about motherhood than the people who run the ranch. In this instance, that wasn't true. A cow should never leave her calf, especially in stormy weather. For this mistake, the cow won herself a trip to the packinghouse, just as soon as the ranch roads were clear of snow.

On ranches, motherhood is taken seriously.

I was able to catch the calf, and we made a home for it in a little hay barn. I gave the calf to Mark, our fourteen-year old son, with the stipulation that he raise it on a bottle and take care of it. We named him Kit, after a friend of ours. The next day we noticed that he was a heifer, so we changed the name to Geraldine, after Kit's wife.

During the cold spell, Mark did a fine job of caring for Geraldine Calf, taking her a warm bottle of milk every morning at daylight and again in the evening. Kids who raise bottle calves are sometimes tempted to increase the ration of milk, because the calves never seem satisfied with one quart.

Mark was wise to that and didn't yield to the temptation, knowing that giving a calf too much milk is the surest way to kill it. It gives them the scours.

After the cold spell passed, Geraldine was doing well. She had grown from an infant into a teenager who could eat some solid food. We decided to move her out of the closed barn and into a wire corral up in Picket Canyon. The next morning, Mark went down to the pen and found it empty. Geraldine Calf had jumped over the fence and wandered away. She was loose somewhere in Picket Canyon—not a good place to be a homeless teenager.

In the afternoon Mark walked up the canyon and tried to summon her with his usual feeding call, a soft two-note "Woo-ooo!"

He came in after dark and his long face gave the report. He hadn't found her and he was beginning to wonder if he ever would.

"Well," I said, "if she doesn't show up in the morning, we'll have to saddle a couple of horses and go looking for her." Mark nodded, but we both knew the odds of our finding a calf in that big rough canyon weren't good. The odds of a pack of coyotes finding her were much better.

We heard the coyotes yapping that evening. They came up close to the house and had our three dogs on Maximum Alert most of the night. I heard them and thought of the calf. I was sure Mark heard them too.

But the next morning at daylight, he looked out the window and saw Geraldine Calf—standing in front of the corral, gazing up at the house and waiting for Mark to come. It was as though she were saying, "Okay, I tried it. You were right. What's for breakfast?"

A Mother Cow

It was a Sunday afternoon in February. Our family had gone into town for church that morning. Kris and the kids stayed in town for church functions in the evening, and I went back to the ranch to feed cattle.

It was along about five in the afternoon when I fed the east pasture. I found the cows in one bunch, at the windmill near the mouth of Point Creek Canyon. I poured out their feed on the ground and walked down the line, counting the cows.

This was calving season and it wasn't unusual for me to come up one or two cows short, but this time I got the full count.

Then I headed west toward Picket Canyon, driving up a steep rocky road that led to some top country. I drove across the flats and was about to take the trail down into Picket Canyon when I noticed something off to my right. At first I thought it might be an antelope, but as I drew closer I saw that it was a baby calf lying in the grass.

I drove over to it and stopped. The calf was alone. I had just fed all the cows in this pasture and had gotten a full count. I knew for a fact that there wasn't a cow within a mile and a half of this little feller, yet here he lay, alone and in plain sight on the bald prairie.

What the heck was he doing here?

Cows don't always take their calves to the feed ground, but why would his momma park him a mile and a half away—on the flats where he could be seen by prowling coyotes? A smart cow would leave her calf in a draw, a few hundred yards from the feed ground, and go back to him as soon as she had eaten. Heck, the cows hadn't grazed this end of the pasture for five days.

Something was wrong here. Things didn't add up. That calf shouldn't have been there, and the next question was, should I intervene? Everything in my experience said, "No, leave it alone." In almost every situation, it's a mistake to disturb a baby calf.

But it was getting along towards sundown and this calf sure looked like coyote bait. I decided to get out of the pickup and approach him. If he jumped up, I would leave. If he allowed me to catch him, then I would haul him down to the herd and turn him loose, hoping that he would find his careless mother.

I approached him one step at a time. He flinched but didn't run, and I was able to grab him. I loaded him into the back of the pickup and tied him down with a lead rope. I drove back to the feed ground and turned him loose among the cows, but before I turned him loose, I bobbed the hair off the end of his tail so that I could identify him.

He bawled. Several cows came over and sniffed him, then walked away. He fell in behind a Hereford-cross cow and followed her away from the feed ground. That looked good—until I identified the cow. Her calf had frozen to death one night when the temperature dropped to twelve below zero, and I knew she was a dry cow.

They didn't belong together, and it began to appear that I should have minded my own business. If the calf's mother was around, she wasn't claiming him, which was very odd.

Well, I didn't know what to do except leave things as they were. If the calf hadn't found his mother by tomorrow, I would have to assume he was abandoned. I would catch him, take him home, and raise him on a bottle.

I headed west again. On reaching the flats, what do you suppose I saw on the horizon? A large four-legged animal trotting towards the southwest end of the pasture. It was Momma Cow, and she was headed straight to the place where she had left her calf—only I had just hauled him a mile and a half to the east.

Mister Smart Guy. Mister Ranch Management Expert.

I drove away, thoroughly humiliated and confident that Mrs. Cow would sort out the mess I had made of her family, if I would just leave. And she did. The next day they were together on the feed ground.

Why had she left him alone, a mile and a half from herself and the other cows? I have no idea, but if the cow knows what she's doing, it isn't necessary for me to understand it.

There's a lesson here, and it's a hard one to remember. No matter how clever we ranchers think we are, none of us knows more about the cow business than a mother cow.

Crazy Jane

Crazy Jane was my name for one of Frankie McWhorter's heifers. Frankie called her other names, which we won't mention.

In November 1987 Frankie began receiving the first of some eight hundred heifers to run on grass on the Gray Ranch. Some were off of the Chapman-Barnard ranch in Osage County, Oklahoma. Others came off the Copeland Ranch in New Mexico. Crazy Jane came with a bunch of Hereford-Brahman crossbreds off a ranch near Marfa, Texas.

In December we spent several days sorting the little darlings by size and color. By the time those heifers reached the Gray Ranch, they hadn't seen too many humans and they all knew how to run. Those that didn't know how to run when they got there soon learned from those snaky little Bramers from South Texas.

I hadn't spent too much time in the company of long-eared cattle and I marveled at their athletic ability. We did some of the cutting ahorseback, holding bunches of two hundred in the corner of a stout fence. We had a good crew and handled them gentle, but even so, they were a challenge

I don't know what kind of horses they use in South Texas, but the ones we used always seemed to be half a step behind those Bramers, who didn't know the meaning of slow and never traveled in singles. When one moved, they all moved, just like minnows.

And they were what you would call hard on pens. We did our gate sorting in the best set of pens I'd ever seen, which Frankie and Roy Tompkins had designed and built from scratch the year before—heavy steel mesh over good pipe, cemented posts, overhead braced corners, gates that latched with sliding steel rods, big pens, plenty of traps nearby.

Those pens were a cowboy's dream. The gate hinges even had grease zerks.

A lesser set of pens wouldn't have survived those heifers. They weren't able to tear them down, but they did leave a bunch of nose prints in that heavy steel mesh, and one of them won herself a trip to the locker plant for her efforts.

When we started the gate sorting, we had ourselves a nice warm December morning. Then a norther came whistling through, bringing clouds and a biting thirty miles an hour wind. The alley ran due north and south. So did the wind. So did the dust.

Say, that was an experience, sorting those world-class sprinters in all that wind and dust. The boys at the south end of the alley, who were swinging the gates and catching the cuts, couldn't see the cattle coming unless they were running faster than the thirty miles an hour dust cloud. Most were.

After we'd sorted them up, we had to drive them to their winter pastures. To say that we "drove" them would be a distortion of what happened. We opened the gates and raced the leaders to the next fence-line, hoping to turn them into a mill before they took out half a mile of fence.

I didn't think those heifers would ever gentle down, but after Frankie had taken them through the winter and spring, they'd become a different set of cattle. He'd spent lots of time riding through them horseback and it sure paid off.

In June Frankie and Dan Cockrell and I did some more sorting on them. We sized them and drove them to summer pastures. That's when Crazy Jane showed her stuff for the first time.

Dan and I had eased a bunch of red baldies out of the sorting trap into a pasture that was just bursting with grass. Most of the heifers wanted to stop and graze, but we pushed them to the water tank.

We rode around them and held them on water for a few minutes, and while we were doing this, a yellow heifer with dark spots around both eyes threw up her head, left the bunch, and trotted off to the south.

I saw her leave, and I knew that we'd have to rope her to get her back. She just had that look about her—the way she carried her head and the expression in her eyes.

Dan galloped after her and turned her towards the fence. I loped out to back him up. I had already taken down my rope and was building a loop.

There was never any question in her mind about what she intended to do when she reached the fence. She didn't hesitate or slow down, just plowed through it and kept right on going, with her head up in the air and her tail curled back into a "figure 9."

Frankie came up about then. With all his heart and soul, he wanted to go after the hussy and give her some private tutoring, but we had more work left to do than daylight, and we had to let her go.

Over the summer Crazy Jane continued to pull stunts that made her stand out from the herd. When Frankie prowled the pasture, she would take off in a run. Since Frankie was doing his best to get the heifers gentled down and accustomed to a horse, this irritated him tremendously. She never quite pushed him to the point of using his rope on her, but she had definitely made herself a marked woman. When we gathered that pasture in September, Frankie was ready for her to pull something.

"We'll do whatever is necessary to keep her with the bunch," he said with an arched brow and a twinkle in his eye. Translation—"If she tries to run, stick a rope on her."

But to everyone's surprise, she didn't make a move. That bunch of crossbred heifers, which had been so unruly back in December, hardly got out of a walk on the two mile drive to the pens.

It appeared that Crazy Jane had changed her ways. But not for long.

When the buyer ran the herd down the alley to make the cuts he had been allowed, it was rather obvious that he didn't want her. While the other heifers trotted past him in orderly fashion, Crazy Jane blew past him like a charging rhinoceros.

She went in the pen with the culls. When we ran the culls through the chute to pregnancy test them, she did her very best to take the head gate out of the chute. She lost that argument, but when she came out of the squeeze, she was in an evil state of mind.

We put in a long hard day, testing several bunches of heifers and shuffling cattle around. The last job of the day was to throw several small bunches of cuts together and then turn them out into a trap for the night. It should have been simple.

Crazy Jane was in with a bunch of eight heifers. Dan Cockrell opened the gate into the trap while Frankie and I went into the pen to drive them out. The other heifers left without any problem. Crazy Jane didn't. She was wild-eyed and snorting by this time, and she started dashing around the pen.

I knew she was stirred up and I knew that she would run over a man if he got in her way. But I didn't expect her to go hunting for someone to run over. I was standing in the middle of the pen, which had plenty of room in it for both of us. She took aim at Frankie but he managed to step out of her path.

I had gotten so involved in watching Frankie that I had forgotten about ME. All at once I realized that eight hundred pounds of mad yellow heifer was bearing down on me from the north. She was moving at a high rate of speed and had one thing on her mind. She had caught me watching the show and it was only a question of how bad the damage would be.

I had no chance to get out of the way, but fortunately I dodged in the right direction. She brushed me with her shoulder, which was plenty enough to lift me off the ground and send me flying south. And down. Yes, lots of down, all of it butt-first, with no chance to roll or break the fall.

The fall might have jarred me worse if I hadn't landed in that big pile of fresh green manure. It sort of greased the skids as I went scooting backwards across the pen.

I collected my hat and sat up.

"Are you hurt?" Frankie managed to ask between chuckles.

"My pride."

"Well, quit stirring up my cattle, and let's get back to work."

Frankie hauled the culls to the livestock auction in Woodward, Oklahoma, and Crazy Jane was bought by a farmer who took her home and added her to his cow herd.

Where is she today? Boy, I'd love to hear that old farmer's stories! I'll bet he has some dandies. My guess is that he spent the next six months chasing her around the county and repairing fence. Then, at his first opportunity, he hauled her right back to the Woodward auction and dumped her off on somebody else.

Some cows aren't a bargain at any price. Crazy Jane was one of those.

Ready to go looking for a wild cow. (L to R): Bobby Barnett, Shay
Pennington, Jason Abraham, Eddy Abraham, and John Erickson (1999)

Red #12

In the spring of 1998 we were gathering the far west pasture and had six cowboys for the job. This wasn't a big pasture, just a tad over 600 acres, but it was a rough rascal and hard to gather. I sent three riders up north to sweep the flat country above the caprock, while the rest of us stayed below the cap and rode out the rolling country and a big sand draw that ran down the middle.

When all the riders had come in, we started pushing the herd toward a small set of wire branding pens in the southeast corner. Lance Bussard rode over to me.

"There was a cow off to herself on top. I couldn't see anything wrong with her, and I don't think she has a calf, but she wouldn't drive. She went to fighting my horse, so I just left her up there. She's got a red ear tag, #12."

I said that was okay. We would be moving the cattle to another pasture in a month or two, and we'd get her then. But when we moved the cattle in August, I looked for Red #12—and she wasn't there. That's when I began to suspect that Red #12 was a solitary cow, one that stayed off to herself and didn't mingle with the rest of the herd.

Over the next several months we caught glimpses of her, but it was always at a time when we were busy with other jobs and couldn't take the time to catch horses and mount a search party. She wasn't hurting anything over there, but it was just a little annoying that she had escaped us twice. I knew we would get her eventually.

In September, Nathan Johnson was helping me on the ranch, and he spotted the cow in the neighbor's pasture. She had found— or had *made*—a hole in the fence and had gone "visitin'," as we say, and that was cause for swift action. Nathan took a horse over to the Wilson place and started driving the cow two miles southeast to the wire pens.

He had trouble driving her, but he managed to get her back into our far west pasture. There, she dived into one of the deep rocky ravines and refused to go any farther.

That was three times. She was building a reputation, and I knew that when we went back the fourth time, we would be armed and dangerous.

The opportunity arose in October, when I had a cowboy crew on the ranch to help us gather and wean calves in the Mesa pasture. After lunch, six of us rode out to find the elusive Red #12. We spread out and covered the country above the caprock. She wasn't there, and we didn't even find fresh tracks.

We made our way down the caprock and rode out the bottom country. There, we found fresh sign that she had been spending time shaded up beneath cedar trees. But when we all converged at a spot near the pens, we had no cow. She had given us the slip again.

Then one of the cowboys, Eddy Abraham from the Canadian, yelled out, "What do you say, John? You give up?" I said yes. Then he pointed to a cedar tree right in front of us. "Well, there she is."

Sure enough, she was standing motionless beneath a cedar tree—right at the point where we had started the gather an hour before! Every one of us had ridden right past the old rip, and she hadn't moved.

When she realized she had been discovered, she blew out of the cedar and tried to make a run to the west, but Eddy got a rope on her and we were able to convince her that she belonged in another pasture.

Red #12 finally got caught by the "long arm of the cowboy," and we put her back with a herd of cows. I wouldn't have bet that she would change her ways, but she did. The following spring, she had a calf, and as far as I know, she hasn't gone back to her solitary habits.

But come to think of it, I haven't seen her in several days.

Part Four

DOGS, CATS, AND 'COONS

Two M-Cross ranch dogs, Texie on the left and Bones (1995)

Bones

One evening several years ago, Scot and Tiffany, our son and daughter-in-law, came out to the ranch for supper. When they pulled up in Scot's pickup, a skinny white dog got out with them. Her name was Bones.

It was nothing new for Scot to show up with a stray dog. He acquired dogs the way dogs acquire fleas. They just appeared. In his growing-up years, Scot kept us well supplied with mongrels, orphans, and vagabonds.

And here was a fresh one, the latest Scot Erickson acquisition. He had found her wandering around on the edge of town, obviously the illegitimate daughter of someone's greyhound. My first impression was...*that is an ugly dog.* She had been well named—Bones.

To my eye, greyhounds are ugly creatures. They look starved, even when they're well fed, and their expressions remind me of vultures. They are bred and trained to chase down animals and kill them, not a particularly cheerful profession, and their expressions reflect it.

When you see four or five of them sticking their heads out of a dog box, you don't want to rush over and pet them.

But the longer I looked at Scot's dog, the less I saw of her "greyhoundness." She was skinny, but not hideously so. A few good meals and a round of worming pills might help. To her credit, she wasn't pure greyhound. Instead of being speckled or some ugly shade of brown, she was pure white, except for a black snip on her tail and a black patch on her face.

And she had a non-greyhound expression. Instead of wearing the grim visage of a buzzard, she had an expression that I could only describe as sweet—big brown eyes, a nicely shaped nose, floppy ears, a kind of smile on her mouth, and a long expressive tail. She gave the impression of being a dog who was happy all the time, a dog with no cares, worries, or problems.

She seemed calm and well mannered, and I could see no sign of neurotic tendencies.

An hour later, as we were sitting out on the porch, I said to Scot, "You know, that's a pretty dog. Why don't you leave her here?"

"Nope."

Half an hour passed. "I like that dog."

"Me too."

Five minutes passed. "Okay, what would you take for her?"

"Hundred bucks."

I got a huge laugh out of that. "Hey Scot, I don't pay money for dogs. I don't *have* to pay money for dogs. They just show up out here."

"She's a good dog."

"She's a mongrel and a stray, and pigs will ride side-saddles before I pay a hundred bucks for a skinny half-greyhound stray dog."

Scot shrugged. "I didn't want to sell her anyway."

There the matter ended. A hundred bucks for a stray dog? Ha! That was outrageous, robbery without a gun. No way, pal.

Scot left that night with my check for a hundred bucks, and I kept his skinny white dog.

It was hard to explain my attraction to Bones. I just liked her. I hope Scot enjoyed his hundred bucks as much as I've enjoyed his dog. It was the best hundred bucks I ever spent. What a deal! I'm just glad he didn't ask for more.

Sophie the Wonder Dog, keeping the M-Cross Ranch safe from
"vampires and monsters" (1994)

Sophie

Sophie came our way in 1989. She was a mixture of two varieties of cowdog, Australian Shepherd and something else. She had bluish-gray and white hair, an intelligent face, a docked tail, and one of those white cowdog eyes.

When we brought her down to the ranch, she took up residence under the bunk house. That seemed a good solution to the housing problem. It got her out of the weather and gave her a place to hide from prowling coyotes.

All went well until we came in for lunch one day. I went inside to build a sandwich, while Sophie wiggled through the crawl space and entered her private domain.

It seems that a skunk had moved in during our absence. I heard barking and growling and supposed she was humbling the cat, which she had to do fairly often.

But then the poisonous vapors began rising from the floor, and I knew what was happening. I grabbed my hat and sandwich and quit the house. Sophie was coming through the crawl space just as I cleared the front porch—an old warped sheet of plywood sitting on four cinder blocks.

The poor old dog must have taken several direct hits. Her eyes were stinging so badly that she could hardly keep them open. She ran to the nearest patch of buffalo grass and began doing dives in it, to rid her coat of the horrible stench.

She coughed and harked for a while, then like a good Marine, went back into combat. Five minutes later she emerged again, gasping for breath and looking through a pair of slit eyes. She made more dives into the grass and went back to work.

I had other things to do and couldn't hang around to watch the finish. It appeared that the battle raged into the afternoon and eventually the skunk moved out—amazed, I would imagine, that his chemical warfare hadn't made more of an impression on this stubborn cowdog.

For the next two days the house was uninhabitable and Sophie had no friends, but she retained possession of her castle. A couple of months went by before she faced another challenge, this time from a 'coon. I had noticed that my dog food bill had shot up for no apparent reason, and when I saw the 'coon tracks in the dust beside the self-feeder, I knew that we had masked bandits on the place.

A few days later I went inside for lunch and had just sat down to enjoy a sauerkraut and salami sandwich, when a terrible racket erupted beneath the floor. This one sounded quite a bit more serious than the skunk episode—barking, growling, screaming, and hissing, as well as the clunking of heads against the floor joists and the clatter of galvanized water pipes.

I shined a flashlight under the house, just to be sure that my dog hadn't tied into a mountain lion or a stray bear. No, it was a 'coon, about half-grown and very noisy. I tried to talk Sophie into giving up the fight, but she wouldn't hear of it.

She stayed submerged for the rest of the day. She fought until both she and the 'coon were exhausted, at which time they rested and glared at each other. Then they went at it again.

I never knew for sure whose head that was, banging against the floor joists, but at least one of them must have come out of it with a serious migraine.

Sometime in the night the 'coon moved out and Sophie became the undisputed ruler of the bunkhouse.

Sophie is like most of the so-called "cowdogs" in our part of the world. She was born with an instinct to do something with cattle but she's never figured out exactly what it is.

We can't blame the dogs entirely for this. The fine print in every dog deal is that you're supposed to *teach* them what to do, and what most of us Rancho-Americans discover is that after teaching children and horses, we have nothing left for the dogs.

It's a bit like buying an exercise bike. To lose weight, you have to ride the silly thing. If the full truth were known about cowdogs and exercise bikes, very few of them would ever be sold.

Nobody wants to ride a bike that doesn't go anywhere, and nobody wants a cowdog who has to be taught how to do his job. As a result, most of the cowdogs in our country end up writing their own job description—and are doomed to a life of comedy.

One of Sophie's most important jobs around here is to shield us from wildlife. Ahorseback in the pasture, we are almost guaranteed never to get a good look at a mule deer or a wild turkey. Patrolling far ahead of us, Sophie will scatter turkeys and chase deer up canyon walls, and though she has been screamed at in several languages, she has never faltered in her duty.

She shows the same determination around the house. I would bet that a gang of burglars could drive a truck up to our house and empty it of furniture, and Sophie would sleep through it all. But let a doe and fawn approach the house and she will come out of a deep sleep, sound the alarm, and go ripping out to chase the intruders away.

Another of her jobs is Monster Watch. Early on, I learned that Sophie studies people. Most dogs I've owned never paid much attention to faces, but Sophie does. When you walk up to her, she watches you, and she's pretty perceptive.

I discovered that if I freeze, she will freeze. If I raise one hand in the shape of a claw, she begins to growl. If I raise a second claw, she will double the volume of her growl. And if I bare my fangs and open my mouth, I can convince her that I have changed into a vampire.

She will stand her ground and bark, unless I happen to lurch forward, and in that case she will take vampire countermeasures and run like a striped ape.

As you might imagine, I have found many opportunities to test her skills. I've learned that her vampire-sensing equipment is so highly developed that I can trigger it just by walking out on the porch and curling my lip at her.

She can pick up vampire signals up to fifty feet away, and even through closed windows. This is very convenient in the winter, as it spares me having to go out into the cold.

The amazing thing about Sophie is that she seems to like me, even though she's convinced that I'm part-monster. We'll play vampires for a while and then I'll smile and say, "Relax, pooch, it's just me." She'll grin and come over for scratches behind the ears, and we'll be friends again.

But the moment I widen my eyes and curl my lip, she's back on the job. She has a special bark for these occasions: "Whuu!" She utters that bark and dashes a safe distance away, where she glares at me and takes up serious growling.

It's as though she's saying, "I knew it! I knew you were a vampire, you can't fool me with that nice-guy routine."

We can do this for hours at a time, going back and forth from vampirism to humanism; day after day, week after week, and I can never convince her that I'm not a closet vampire.

Well, that is what my cowdog does for a living, and to be fair about it, I guess she's been pretty successful. We've been on this ranch for ten years and nobody has ever been attacked by a deer or a turkey—or a vampire.

Penny

Penny was a sweet little dog. She came to us from our neighbors up on the flats. Her father was a Border Collie named Tex, and Tex was an expert at chasing a Frisbee. He would race after a Frisbee, leap high into the air, and snag it in his mouth.

We had hopes that Penny would follow in the old man's foot-steps, but when we got her down to the ranch and tossed a Frisbee, she showed no interest in it.

But a few days later, Mark and I were throwing a football in front of the house, and Penny came to life. All at once she became Charles Haley, the best pass-rushing dog in Roberts County.

Mark and his pals spent many pleasant hours playing keep-away with Penny. She would follow the ball wherever it went, and woe be unto the quarterback who had a slow release. If Penny couldn't get to the ball, she would often settle for the quarterback's bellybutton. She sent several boys back to town with red tattoos on their mid-sections.

I always thought it was odd that a football triggered something in her mind—not a stick or a sock or a Frisbee or something sensible, but a football which she could never have the satisfaction of seizing in her jaws.

Maybe it was related to her fixation on birds. Why would a pooch with cowdog breeding bark at birds? I have no idea, but she was nutty about birds. She would chase and bark at them for hours, sometimes in the middle of the night.

When Penny joined our outfit, she became second-dog to Sophie, who had been with us for five years. It was interesting to watch the pecking order as it unfolded.

Sophie seemed to have mixed feelings about the new pup. On the one hand, Sophie had a companion on the ranch, but on the other hand, Penny was a constant source of irritation. For the first time in her life, Sophie found herself competing for attention.

The football games were especially hard on Sophie, since she had no aptitude for sports. While Penny chased the ball, Sophie would chase Penny, barking in a neurotic frenzy and occasionally throwing her to the ground.

Sophie also found herself competing for scraps with a dog that was smaller, younger, and quicker than she. As soon as the scraps left the plate and hit the ground, Sophie's first move was to freeze Penny with a snarl. Only then would she dive on the scraps.

Penny compensated for this by developing a lightning grab. Any time a foreign object came off the porch and hit the ground, she would come flying out of nowhere and wolf it down, then flee before Sophie knew what had happened.

This led to some real comedy. One day I went to the house for lunch. On the porch, I paused to pitch a quid of chewing tobacco out into the yard. In a flash, Penny was there and gulped it down.

On another occasion, I found a hunk of dried cat manure on the porch. I tossed it out into the yard. Seconds after it hit the ground, Penny gobbled it down.

Mark, who was eleven and a curious lad, wondered just how far Penny would take this exercise. One day he threw a small caliche rock out the door, and sure enough, Penny ate it.

If she had worms, they must have thought they were living in an insane asylum.

Although Sophie hated to share food and attention, she soon figured out that there were advantages to having a pup on the place. Penny could take over the job of raising Mark. Both youngsters had thermonuclear sources of energy, and Sophie was beginning to feel her age.

So while Mark and Penny romped in the yard, wrestled on the porch, and hiked through the canyons, Sophie eased into semi-retirement and began spending more time sleeping in a certain padded chair on the front porch.

Many a time I saw her there and felt a common bond, and many a time I joined her in the next chair. Together, we sat and mused about the tricks that Time doth play on us all.

There's another story about Penny and Sophie, and it's a strange one.

One morning around sunrise, Penny got run over. It's not easy for a dog to get run over on our place. We're at the end of the county road, forty miles from town, and our traffic on an average day consists of maybe five ranch and oil field pickups, driving at less than twenty miles an hour.

But she did it. In the darkness before daylight, she darted out in front of Don Malone's pickup. He never saw her, just heard a thump. She lived long enough to crawl out into the horse pasture, and there she died.

The strange part is that we had trouble finding the body. The kids and I knew she was there, but we had to walk and search for half an hour before we found her. At last we looked under a pile of grass and twigs—and there was Penny.

This baffled me. Who or what had taken the time to cover a dead pup with leaves and twigs, and had done such a thorough job of it that we had walked past it several times? After eliminating all other possibilities, I concluded that Sophie had done it.

Why would a dog do such a thing? We humans would cover the body of a friend with a sheet. We'd do it out of love and respect, for we understand that in death we are helpless, and that we are not pretty in our last hours.

But that is a fairly sophisticated response. It requires a sense of one's own mortality, and dogs, we assume, don't have that. Or do they? One of the things that makes dogs such a fascinating study is that their behavior often leaves us puzzled.

Dogs spend a high percentage of their time doing things that, to us, seem moronic and pointless. They can be such fools and yet, they have this other side which has made them man's best friend for uncounted centuries, and you won't find it in a chicken, a cat, or a horse. In rare moments, dogs are capable of rising above their role as clown and fool, and they can demonstrate a level of perception that is almost spooky.

In a glance, they read our faces and know our thoughts. Without the exchange of a single word, they share whatever emotion they find in our eyes. Stories abound of dogs that answered a moment of crisis with courage that any human would be proud to imitate.

Dogs occupy an emotional space that is exceeded only by man's, and they are capable of running through the entire spectrum, from utter stupidity to selfless devotion, in just a matter of minutes.

I don't know why Sophie covered Penny's body. I never heard of a dog doing such a thing. Did she think that Penny was just an extra large bone, or did she have some faint understanding that her friend had gone away?

That night we were sitting out on the porch, Sophie and I. When I whispered, "Where's Penny?" she turned her head and wouldn't look at me.

Oh, and by the way, in 1999 when Bones died of a rattlesnake bite, I found her body—covered with sticks and weeds, just as Penny's had been.

It makes me wonder.

Texie, The Incredible Burping Dog

After Penny's demise, we acquired a dog named Texie. She was a small black and white dog with a stub tail. Her coloring suggested some Border Collie breeding. Her intelligence suggested that she came from a line of fence posts.

This dog is not only dumb but also disobedient. When you call her, she slinks away. When you raise your voice to call her again, she runs away. When you chase her, she hides. When you finally get your hands on her, she is so stricken with guilt and fear that she loses her bladder control.

She knows only one trick, and I must admit that it's pretty impressive. She's the only dog I ever knew who burps. Now, a normal ranch dog will burp after drinking a lot of water or wolfing down a plate of scraps. That's not what we're talking about. Texie burps *all the time.*

I can't reproduce the sound with English words. It doesn't come out as "burp," "urp," "bork," or "ump." It's an inhuman sound, something between the croak of a frog and the squeak of a rusty hinge.

She does it quite often, and it's *loud*. You can hear it from one end of the front porch to the other. When we have visitors, we have to explain that we don't have alligators, it's just Texie the Incredible Burping Dog.

Most visitors are amused. Like us, they have never known a dog that made such weird noises.

The great mystery is that our son Mark cares for this dog. He forgives her for being a disobedient little weenie. They go hiking together in the canyon and naturally, he's proud that she can out-burp any dog in Roberts County. It was because of Mark's affection for Texie that I decided not to murder her several months ago.

I had sent Mark on some errand in the evening, to feed some horses or shut off a water well. As usual, he chose to drive my new Ford pickup. After driving junk pickups most of my life, I had finally paid the price to buy a new one. It was a heck of a price but a heck of a good pickup, with nice seats and interior.

Mark took Texie with him, of course, and she rode in the jump seat in the back. Off they went, a thirteen year old ranch kid and his faithful burping dog. They made quite a pair.

I am guessing that on the way back home, Mark slipped a Chris LeDoux tape into the tape player and was lost in thoughts of "Bareback Jack" or some other rodeo song, and when he shut off the pickup and got out, he forgot about Texie.

She spent the night in my $28,000 pickup.

What did she do? Not what you think. It was worse. She chewed both upholstered door panels and one arm rest into *shreds!*

When I opened the pickup door the next morning, I saw ribbons of cloth hanging from the doors. Then I saw Texie and looked into her vapid eyes. Her expression said, "It wasn't me, honest." Then she burped.

Who can murder such an animal?

I threw her out, fumed at Mark for fifteen minutes, and made it clear that his pickup-eating dog could walk from now on. For the next two months we drove around in a shredded pickup. In July I had to take it to town and get some work done on it, so I told the service manager to fix the interior.

Would anyone like to buy the Incredible Burping Dog? I've got seven hundred bucks invested in her, but I'd probably take six and a half.

Callie Cat

If she had been a dog, you would have called her a mongrel. She was a brindle-colored cat, and one day she showed up at our house in town.

She was gentle and had a sweet disposition, but we weren't exactly in the market for a cat. We had two already, a male and a female, and that mix promised to keep us in the cat business for a long time.

No, we didn't need another cat to feed in town, but it happened that I had just found evidence of mice in the saddle house at the ranch. They had just about eaten the straps off of Scot's breast harness, and had started working on his cinch latigo.

So the next time we went to the ranch, we hauled Callie Cat with us and introduced her to her new home.

I didn't know whether Callie Cat would survive on the ranch or not. Our country is rather wild and rugged, and well populated with certain furry creatures of the night that are known to have a taste for kitties.

I'm speaking of coyotes, of course. A cowboy friend of mine once observed that the tricks cats use to intimidate dogs simply don't work on coyotes. A cat seems to have no good defense against the coyote, and for that reason ranch cats, not coyotes, have become an endangered species on Panhandle ranches.

But I wished her the best. If she could thin out the mice and discourage rattlesnakes from coming up around the bunkhouse, she would have a permanent job on our outfit.

One day Mark and I killed a diamondback and took it to the bunkhouse. Mark wanted to skin him out and preserve the skin. The snake was lying in the front yard, and I watched Callie to see what she would do.

Here was a town cat that had never seen a snake before, and I wondered if she had a natural fear of it.

She certainly did. The snake was still twisting and moving, even though his head was off in the pasture, and Callie approached him with equal amounts of caution and curiosity.

I couldn't resist tossing a stick in her direction, and couldn't resist laughing when she sprang two feet straight up in the air.

The weeks stretched into months, and Callie was still with us. She seemed to understand that her survival depended on sticking close to civilization. A tomcat might have gotten restless and wandered away, but Callie made her camp under the porch or in the stock trailer nearby.

Her closest brush with death came, not from prowling coyotes, but from a friend of mine named Henry Hale. Henry and I had gone into the bunkhouse for lunch one day, and Callie managed to slip in with us.

While Henry was building himself a baloney sandwich, Callie hopped up on the dinner table and then launched herself onto Henry's neck. She came very close to getting herself stabbed with a table knife.

But all good things come to an end. One day in August, Ashley and Mark and I drove over to the east pasture and stopped on the rim of a deep canyon. I had warned the kids not to take Callie with us when we drove around the ranch, for while a dog will come to a call, a cat won't.

Sure enough, they had taken Callie for a ride, and sure enough, she hopped out of the Jeep. By the time we saw her, she was making her way down a sheer rock face of Point Creek Canyon, and heading for the dense cedars at the bottom.

If we had been carrying five catch ropes, we might have been able to tie them together and lower Mark down to retrieve her. But we weren't and we couldn't, and I told the kids to blow their goodbye kisses to Callie Cat, because we would never see her again.

That canyon was two rugged miles and several dozen coyotes from the house, and there was no way a dinky little town cat could find its way back.

And that was the end of it.

Miracles do happen—two weeks later, Callie Cat showed up at the bunkhouse.

She was either the smartest—or the luckiest—cat in Roberts County.

Eddy the Rac, with John Erickson (1990)

Eddy the Rac

One day in July 1992, Mark and I were hiking around Picket Canyon. Sophie the Wonderdog went with us, of course, and when we came to a dry pond, she disappeared into a patch of tall sunflowers. We heard her barking at something.

Sophie wasn't inclined to bark without a reason, so we figured she had found a snake, a porcupine, or a skunk. I climbed on top of a big rock where I could see into the sunflowers. I saw something move down below. I looked closer and saw a small raccoon, maybe half-grown.

I knew what Sophie had in mind for that little 'coon. I pulled on the work gloves I had been carrying in my pocket, crawled down the side of the rock, and plucked the little fellow out of the sunflowers.

He let out a squall and tried to bite me, but within an hour he had settled down and I was carrying him around on my shoulder. I was amazed. Some years ago I had tried to make pets out of several coyote pups and they had never lost their wildness. But this little guy adjusted to us right away and seemed comfortable about it.

I had known people who had raised pet 'coons and I had always wanted to try it myself. I knew the kids would enjoy him, and I had reason to think that a pet 'coon would make an interesting character for a Hank the Cowdog book.

We decided to call him Eddy. Eddy the Rac.

Eddy was old enough to eat solid food, but when we offered him bits of weenie, crackers, and bread, he showed no interest. Then we remembered that the wild plums were in season. We picked a batch and offered him one. His eyes brightened. He took the ripe plum in his hands, rolled it around, and nibbled it down to the seed.

The next day Mark and Ashley went for a swim in a stock tank. They took Eddy along and he enjoyed the water as much as they. Mark noticed some polliwogs in the water, caught one, and held it in front of Eddy's nose. That really brought him to life. He snatched it away and gobbled it down.

For the next several weeks, one of Mark and Ashley's daily chores was catching polliwogs for Eddy. There seem no limit to his appetite for them.

We offered him other kinds of food from our refrigerator and he showed no interest in them. Except bananas. He loved bananas, and we got many laughs watching him smack his way through a hunk of banana. I thought it was odd that a 'coon from the Texas Panhandle showed no interest in apples or pears, but had a strong appetite for a fruit grown in the tropics.

At first we kept Eddy in the bathtub. This was a tub with a shower head and sliding glass doors. When we closed the doors, we assumed he couldn't get out. Ha. He got out the first night and it took us an hour to find him. He had opened one of the drawers in the bathroom and was curled up asleep, beside the toothpaste and dental floss.

We soon realized that 'coons don't sleep at night and can escape from anything. Eddy seemed driven to get out of wherever he was, so that he could go someplace that seemed, to us, no better than the first location.

It was just his nature. He was a little Houdini, born to escape and wander.

That finally got him into trouble. We had moved him out of the bathroom and into a rabbit cage in the back yard of our house in town. It didn't take him long to pick the lock, and one morning we found the cage empty. This time, Eddy was gone for good. We could only hope that his urge for freedom didn't get him involved with someone's dog.

Days passed. No Eddy. Then one evening we got a call from Donnie, our next-door neighbor. "Don't y'all have a pet 'coon?" Yep, used to. "Well, I think I know where he is. He's in Booker."

Booker! Booker was a small town sixteen miles east of Perryton. We'd always known that Eddy was a rambler, but how could he have gotten all the way to Booker? Here's how it happened—

When Eddy broke out of the rabbit cage, he wandered over to Donnie's house and crawled up under the hood of his car. He must have stayed there for several days, then Donnie drove the car over to a mechanic in Booker to get some work done. Eddy went along.

The car sat there for another day or two before the mechanic opened the hood and started working on the motor. At some point Eddy appeared, and no doubt the mechanic got the shock of his life.

Anyway, we got Eddy back. He stayed with us for a few more weeks, but he seemed so determined to wander that we decided to let him go. That happens with 'coons and teenagers.

He was an interesting little friend, and if you happen to read books #20, #24, and #32 in the Hank the Cowdog series, you'll meet a character named Eddy the Rac. He's a little con artist, and Houdini when it comes to getting out of cages.

Part Five

HORSES

Reno

When I was cowboying in Beaver County, Oklahoma in the 1970s, I rode a sorrel gelding named Reno. He was half-Arabian and half-Quarter Horse. He had the quickness and agility of a Quarter Horse and the endurance of an Arabian, and boy, that rascal was the king when it came to chasing wild cattle through the sandhills north of the Beaver River.

He had two gears: Park and Wide-open. When he shifted out of Park, you'd better have a deep seat because you had your saddle on a tornado. In the four years I rode him he never bucked, but sometimes it was hard to tell. After a day on Reno, I had so many saddle galls on my legs that I had to bandage my wounds in order to ride him the next day.

Reno had the courage of a lion and I developed a deep admiration for him, but we never became what you would call "friends." He wasn't an affectionate horse. Strictly business, that was Reno. If you could catch him in the corral, if you could stay on his back in the pasture, he'd give you his body and soul. But between jobs, he was remote.

I considered him a hero. I don't know what he thought of me, but "tolerance" would probably describe his attitude. To do his job, to be a star out in the pasture, he needed me.

One day in 1976 we were helping Mark Mayo gather his cattle on the Beaver River. We had penned the herd and had begun sorting off the cows. Reno and several other horses were tied to the fence. Two big horned Hereford bulls began scuffling, and it developed into a serious fight. Dust rose in the air and cowboys headed for safer ground. All at once, one of the bulls turned to run and smashed right into the horses. They screamed and sent reins and headstalls flying in pieces as they scrambled out of the path of the bull.

Reno didn't get out of the way soon enough, and the bull drove his horn six inches into the base of Reno's throat. As the dust began to clear, I saw him. A broken headstall hung from one ear and blood spurted from his wound.

It was obvious that the horn had cut into his jugular vein and that he was bleeding to death. He walked with short wobbly steps and he came straight towards me. For a few seconds everything around me receded into the background and I was aware only of Reno's eyes. I think he knew he was mortally wounded and he didn't want to die alone.

Was I imposing human thoughts and feelings on a horse? I don't think so. It was one of those moments when everything was clear. Reno, the aloof professional, didn't want to bleed to death around strangers.

Well, he didn't bleed to death. Quick action by Mark saved him. Mark used his hands to apply pressure on the vein and sent someone to the house to call the vet. Four or five of us took turns putting pressure on the vein until Doc Chockley arrived forty minutes later, and by then the bleeding had stopped.

The horn had torn a small hole in the vein. If it had entered a fraction of an inch to one side, we wouldn't have been able to save the horse.

Would you believe that after this near-death experience, Old Reno changed his attitude and that we became the best of pals? Ha. No, he healed up and a month later he was back on the job, chasing wild cows in the sandhills. And his attitude toward me remained the same: if I could catch him, he would work; if I couldn't, too bad.

The Ericksons and their Arabians. (L to R): Ashley Erickson on Nocona, Mark Erickson on Calipso, and John Erickson on Dandy (1992)

Calypso

Calypso was foaled in May 1975 on a ranch in Beaver County, where I was working as a cowboy. She was out of a good Arabian stallion and a soured old Thoroughbred racehorse mare.

I started breaking her to ride when she was two. I rode her bareback at first, as I got acquainted with her moods and temperament. She was a sweet little mare, but she had enough of that Thoroughbred blood in her to be a little unpredictable at times. And she did manage to stick my nose into a few sandhills.

In 1977 I started working Wednesday afternoons at the Beaver Livestock Auction, penning cattle in the yards when they came off the scales. This was a way of making a little extra money, and it was also an excellent place to train a colt.

I thought the stockyard work would be good experience for Calypso, teach her to watch a cow. It did.

I penned a few cattle on her that first day and they all played by the rules, but then we fell in behind an old crooked-horn, mottle-face cow that had been choused about as many times that day as she cared to be choused.

She came off the scales with a bad attitude. We didn't have to do anything to get her on the hook. She was already there—which probably had a lot to do with her being sold.

She went streaking down the alley. Bobby Woodson and his horse Yeller were at the proper pen and had the gate opened. Old Crooked Horn blew into the pen, checked it out real fast, and came back into the alley, saying, "No thanks, guys."

Bobby threw the gate into her face, which would have turned most cows of sound mind, but it only made Crooked Horn a little madder at the world.

And here she came back up the alley, headed straight for me and Calypso.

My little mare hadn't seen too many cows of any kind, and she had never seen one that had murder on her mind. She threw up her ears, skidded to stop, swapped ends, took the bit in her teeth, and bucked the entire length of that alley, while Crooked Horn breathed hot vapors on her tail section and Bobby squalled, "Ride 'er, John, point them toes!"

That was derned sure the best ride I ever made. I probably couldn't have done it out in the pasture, but there in the stockyards, with wooden pens on both sides and a psychopathic cow on the loose, I wasn't about to get bucked off.

We survived that deal, but for the next month, every time a cow looked hard at Calypso, I had a riot on my hands.

Dandy

Dandy was an Arabian gelding. I bought him as a six-year old in the fall of 1990.

By the time I had ridden him four or five times, I thought I had him pretty well figured out. He had tremendous endurance and raw athletic ability, but he didn't know how to use them.

He had no finish, no finesse. He had never learned to control himself or to direct his physical gifts into productive channels:

A bomb and a pickup motor draw upon the same principles of physics. Both involve an explosion, but the motor is engineered to control the energy and use it to accomplish a task.

Dandy appeared to be more of a bomb than a motor. By that, I don't mean to imply that he was a bucking horse. He wasn't, but sometimes it was hard to tell if he was bucking or just moving in his normal manner.

He was an explosive horse and just staying in the saddle with him was a challenge. After riding Dandy, a guy didn't need to visit an amusement park.

I figured that our ranch in the Canadian River valley would take a lot of that high octane out of him. It was a rough old ranch, with plenty of up-and-down, and I felt sure that the country would teach him a few lessons about the conservation of energy.

I found out pretty quickly that he had more endurance than I had ranch. I could get him tired, and I mean dripping sweat and heaving for air, but then he would take a couple of deep breaths and he'd be ready to go again.

A normal day of rounding up cattle was just a warm-up for Dandy. To slow him down and get his attention, I had to take him to the sand draw before the work started and try to ride him into the ground.

After we had galloped figure-eights in deep sand for twenty minutes, he was about ready to start the day's work.

After I'd worked with Dandy for two years, I began to suspect that he would never amount to much as a ranch horse. He just had no interest in cow work. Sure, he was a great athlete, but another name for great athlete is "dumb jock."

The last straw came at the next spring roundup. A little part-Bramer calf broke out of the corral and I needed to rope him. I knew that Dandy was about as sorry a roping horse as there was in the country, but the job needed to be done.

I unlatched my twine, loaded up, and gave Dandy his head. He hit the jets and caught up with the calf in a matter of seconds, blew past him and ran right through the middle of a mesquite bush. I don't think he even knew the calf was there.

On the other side of the mesquite bush, as I searched for my stirrups and dignity, I realized that Dandy and I weren't in the same business, and never would be. He was a great athlete who was wasting his talent on my place.

A few months later I traded him to a man who made long endurance rides. He thought Dandy would be a natural for that line of work. He seemed to have been born for it.

I guess Dandy had tried to tell me that. A guy could sure save himself a lot of grief if, every once in a while, he tried listening to his horse.

Tom

I acquired Tom in a horse trade. He was a handsome slick-haired sorrel gelding. I got him cheap and was proud of myself—until I found out why he was cheap.

One day in August, I decided to take the family out for a ride. I put Kris on old Snips. Ashley rode her mare, Nocona. Mark rode Calypso, and cousin Kristi rode Tolstoy.

I rode Tom. I wanted to show him off to the family.

After saddling all the horses, I told the kids to mount up, check their stirrups, and warm up their horses in the corral. I figured I might as well warm up Tom, even though I was pretty sure he didn't need it.

I stepped into the left stirrup and swung up. In the blink of an eye, I found myself draped across Tom's neck, and he was bucking around the corral.

At such moments, you become aware of all the objects in a corral that you wouldn't want to meet head-on—large cedar posts, stock tanks, landing mats, gates, and saddle sheds.

I hoped to miss most of them, but there wasn't much I could do about it. I was well beyond the advice of Jim Shoulders to "keep a leg on each side and your mind in the middle."

This was no bronc ride. It was an embarrassment. I was a sack of potatoes on a streak of lightning, and I was lucky to come off when and where I did.

I got up and dusted myself off. I noticed several children biting back smiles. Tom bucked two laps around the pen and stopped. I leveled a finger at him and said, "Okay, buddy, we're going to the sand draw."

We have this place in the middle of the Mesa pasture, a draw of deep sand. I call it Erickson's Sand Draw School For Wayward Horses. I use it to fulfill my number one rule: *After the age of 35, never get into a fair fight with a horse.*

The theory is simple. A horse that will buck on tight ground will think twice about bucking in deep sand. If he does buck, he will be shooting blanks instead of cannon balls. If he succeeds in unhorsing his past-thirty-five year old rider (husband, father of three, sole wage earner and payer of taxes), the damage will be slight.

In the middle of the sand draw, I thrust a booted foot into the stirrup, swung my right leg over the saddle—and found myself sprawled across his neck again, as he went bucking off to the east.

It was the same deal, a sack of potatoes, but the sand was softer than the dirt in the corral. I'd gotten that part right.

Kris and the kids caught the horse and led him back. I could hear my teeth grinding together. Smoke began to curl out of both nostrils.

"Okay, buddy, you did it twice. Let's see you do it three times."

Maybe I should have chosen different words, because he did it again, and made it look pretty easy. I was mad enough by then to eat nails and bite huge trees in half.

I finally rode him the fourth time. By then he must have been tired or bored.

In the hours and days that followed this debacle, I found myself wondering—how did I end up on his neck, for Pete's sake? That was a totally new experience for me.

Then a friend pointed out the obvious. When a guy ends up around his horse's neck, it means that the horse is moving *backward* during the mounting process. It can't happen any other way, and when it happens three times in a row, it's no accident.

Why, the dirty, low-down, back-stabbing—he had ambushed me three times in a row, and I'd been too dumb to figure out what he was doing.

I spent many hours plotting a solution to his treachery. I considered using hobbles and ropes and various horse-breaking tricks. Then I consulted a friend who was wiser than I, and he came up with the answer.

"Sell 'im."

I did, and it was one of the best horse-breaking techniques I'd ever used.

Sinbad

I made a horse-swap in the spring of 1993. I traded an eight-year old gelding for a six-year old gelding, plus a yearling colt called Sinbad.

I thought that was pretty shrewd of me, getting two horses for one. It was probably the best horse deal I'd ever made.

I had been warned that the colt was a little hellion mustang, sired by a wild stallion that ran on Bureau of Land Management property in Montana. An intelligent being would have taken that as a warning, but I took it as a challenge. Patience and a few wet blankets would work wonders.

As I watched Sinbad unload from a two-horse trailer, I began to wonder. He tried his best to dismantle the trailer and stack the pieces. Fortunately, he came with a halter and lead rope already installed.

Oh well, I figured this would be an adventure. It was.

After three days of trying, I was able to grab the lead rope. Within a week, I could lead him around without a tractor. In only a month, he allowed me to touch him.

It was slow but I could see progress. I tried to work with him twice a day. He came along. After three months I could run my hand over his back, under his belly, and down his legs. I could touch him everywhere...except his ears.

I was sharp enough to realize that this could cause problems down the line. Ranch horses need to be bridled, and it's hard to bridle a horse that won't stand to be touched on the ears.

I tried to be patient, but Sinbad was very stubborn about it. Days melted into weeks, and I found myself becoming resentful. Every time I poured out his feed, I felt my patience ebbing away.

At last, one evening in August, I decided the time had come to be firm with the little snipe. After all, I was the horse trainer, the ranch owner, and the guy who paid the feed bill.

It was time for Junior to give up his ears. I forced the issue in the presence of two of my children. I wanted to contribute to their education. I did.

I went through the usual warm-up with the colt, working my way towards the Forbidden Ears. He knew what was coming and tried to put his head out of reach.

Before, I hadn't pressed the issue. This time I did.

I never dreamed that a colt could strike in the blink of an eye, but he did. I never saw it coming, never suspected a thing.

One second, I was saying, "Now kids, I'm going to—" And the next second, my hat and glasses were twenty-five feet away. I was standing on wobbly legs, thinking that part of my face was rolled up and lying at my feet.

"He struck me," I said to the children, who were staring at me with eyes as big as biscuits.

Ashley nodded. "And you're bleeding."

My fingers traced out the path of damage: a lump on the top of my head, skidmarks down my forehead, and a deep two-inch gash on my left eyebrow. But the rest of the face was intact, which came as a relief.

I learned several lessons from this experience.

Lesson One: Your average horse can pull a gun quite a bit faster than most aging cowboy/authors can dodge.

Lesson Two: When you buy stitches thirteen at a time, they run about twenty-five bucks apiece.

Lesson Three: He who punches the Payer of the Feed Bill will soon get shipped. I didn't even try to sell him. I *gave* him to Katherine Paul in Lipscomb County. If anyone could find the good in a young horse, it was Katherine.

And she did. After working with him for a year, she managed to gentle him down, and she found a home for him with a family in Oklahoma. "They think he's the most wonderful horse in the world," Katherine told me, "and he's being ridden by a little girl."

Well, that kind of wounded my pride, but after thinking about it for a while, I decided that things had turned out just right.

In fact, giving that little bronc away was the best horse deal I'd ever made. He'd found a good home—and there's no telling how much money I'd saved on doctor bills.

Sabalita

One day in the summer of 1995, I went into the lumber yard to buy some fencing material. I was standing at the counter, waiting to sign the ticket, when Alan Randall, the manager, came over to me.

"I hear you like Arabian horses. I've got one you need to buy." And he told me the story of how he happened to own a sorrel Arabian mare.

A friend of his bought the mare for his wife, but then learned that he had been transferred. He had to leave on short notice, couldn't take the mare, and didn't have time to sell her. If Alan didn't buy her, he would have to take her to a horse sale, which probably meant that she would end up as pet food.

Alan didn't need another horse to feed, especially an Arabian. He was a Quarter Horse man. But he looked at the mare. She was a beautiful thing, tall and lithe, who moved with all the dignity of the Arabian breed.

He couldn't bear the thought of such a beautiful animal going to the killer plant, so he bought her for six hundred bucks.

"I've kept her for a year and have hardly ridden her," Alan told me. "I've got too many horses and she's got to go. She's six years old and gentle. I'll sell her for $650."

I told Alan I would think about it, but I already knew my answer. I had seven horses down at the ranch and that was all we needed for our cattle work. I just let it drop.

Six months later I ran into Alan again. "John, I'm going to sell that mare. Nobody around here rides Arabians, and if you don't buy her, I'm going to haul her to the next horse sale. That would be a real shame."

"Alan, I don't need the mare. I don't want the mare. I've got all the bad habits I can afford right now."

He shook his head. "That's too bad. She's a beauty, and a heck of a bargain."

I thought it over. "Tell you what. I've got a filly that's green-broke and needs some riding. I never seem to get around to it. You ride my filly for thirty days and I'll buy the mare."

It was a deal.

The first weekend in October, Alan drove down to the ranch with Sabalita in his trailer. I saddled her up and walked her around the pen, then kicked her up into a trot. I pulled her up to a stop, reined her left and right, then trotted her out again.

Well, she had passed her first test. It didn't mean that she would ever make a good ranch horse. It would take a while to determine that. But I had seen enough to know that she was worth the selling price.

I wrote Alan a check for the mare, and he went back to town. I found myself admiring my new acquisition. She was indeed a beautiful animal and she had an unusually fine head, set on a long curved Arabian neck. Her legs were long and straight. Her coat was shiny and she was in good shape, yet she didn't carry any extra flesh.

She seemed to have a calm disposition. She didn't appear nervous about being in a new place. Rather, she was very curious.

She put her nose to the ground and smelled out the whole corral, just as a dog would have done it. I couldn't remember ever seeing a horse do that.

Beauty and intelligence were good qualities to have in a ranch horse, but they weren't enough to win her a permanent place on our outfit. This was a working cow ranch and our horses were tools, not art objects. Any horse that stayed on our place would have to work hard. If Sabalita didn't have courage and an appetite for work, she wouldn't be around for long, no matter how pretty she was.

What I knew of Sabalita's background told me that she had never been worked. Nobody had demanded much out of her. She had spent most of her six years taking life easy, grazing in a grass paddock.

Tomorrow I would take her to the sand draw, and there I would find out who she was.

One of the things that fascinates me about horses is that, in certain respects, they are very similar to humans. I don't mean that they *are* human or that we should hug them and fuss over them and turn them into surrogate babies. But there are points of similarity.

One trait we have in common is that *character* is the defining quality in both of us. A person with good character is honest and courageous, and the same is true of a horse. At the core of every horse and human, there is a mysterious something that defines who we are and how we respond to a challenge or crisis.

My early impression of Sabalita was that she appeared to be honest, but I wasn't sure about her courage. Courage—or "heart," as horse people often call it—is a very important quality in a ranch horse and it isn't something that shows up right away. It's an inner quality that has little to do with size, color, or breed.

My experience is that horses reveal this side of their character when they get tired. A gutless horse will quit. One with "heart" will find a way to keep going.

Over the past five years, I had owned two horses that proved to be gutless. Both were handsome brutes. But in both cases, when they reached a certain level of fatigue, they simply quit, as though they were operating on a time clock. If I spurred them, they would sull or try to buck.

Those horses didn't stay around here very long. Maybe a better horse trainer could have gotten more out of them, but I couldn't. I sold them.

And that's what I had to find out about Sabalita—if she had the strength of character to make a contribution to our ranch, which is very rough and demanding of horseflesh.

The day after she arrived, I loaded her in the stock trailer and hauled her down to the sand draw. It is an area of deep sand in a bend of Picket Ranch Creek, and this is where I study the character of colts and new horses.

The sand serves two purposes. First, it saps a horse of energy two or three times faster than hard ground and accelerates the "discovery" process. This is handy with Arabian horses, since their endurance can sometimes wear out the rider before the horse. Second, if a guy gets himself bucked off, the sand is two or three times softer than firm ground.

I took Sabalita into the sand and began walking her through circles and figure-eights. I didn't wear spurs in the early going, because I didn't know whether she had ever been ridden with spurs or how she might respond.

We walked and trotted for about fifteen minutes. She was soft and out of shape, and she soon showed a sweat. And she quit. I thumped her sides with my boot heels, but she refused to move.

"Well," I thought, "I have just bought myself another gutless horse." But to be sure, I strapped on my spurs and tried again. When she felt the spurs, her ears shot up and she wrung her tail. I waited for her to buck or sull, but she didn't. She moved out in a brisk trot.

This gave me some insight into her background. It told me that she had never been asked to do much. Her previous owners had ridden her until she got tired and then had put her back in her stall. She had never been pushed and she had no knowledge of her limits.

It was as though a light had come on in her mind. "Oh. You mean I don't have to quit when I get tired? You think I can do more? Well, maybe I can."

The next time I took her to the sand draw, I pushed her a little harder. We trotted figure-eights in the deep sand until she broke a sweat. She let me know that she wanted to quit, but I nudged her with the spurs and she kept going.

Then I kicked her up into a lope. I could be wrong, but I got the impression that she didn't know that she could lope under saddle. Perhaps her previous owners had never gotten her out of a trot.

After thirty minutes, I was so pleased with her responses that I decided to leave the sand draw and ride out into the pasture. There was some risk in taking her out of a controlled environment where she was doing well, and into one where she would encounter objects and sounds that were strange to her.

In training a horse, you have to try to see the world through the mind and eyes of a horse. This mare had spent her life in stalls and paddocks. I was taking her out into a pasture where every object was new and strange to her.

There were rocks in the pasture. She had never seen a rock before. We rode through wild plum thickets and tall grass, both of which scratched her on the flanks. She had never felt that before. We crossed a boggy spot where the windmill overflowed. Perhaps she had never walked through mud. We traveled over ditches, washed-out cow trails, and ravines, none of which had been part of her experience.

She faced each of these things with suspicion—stopped, nickered, and studied it with eyes, ears, and nose. Only then did she proceed. With each one, she gained confidence in her ability to travel over broken ground, and she also gained confidence in me, that I was not asking her to do things that were dangerous or impossible.

We rode the Mesa pasture for two hours. She did fine.

I was ready to take her to the next level and let her experience a cattle roundup. It happened that our fall roundup was scheduled for the next day. I hadn't supposed that Sabalita would be ready to use in the roundup, but I was so pleased with her progress that, on the spur of the moment, I decided to ride her the first day. That was a compliment to her.

We gathered two pastures that day. The cattle in both pastures were wild and hard to handle, and I had to push the mare well beyond the limits we had explored in our early rides. She rose to the challenge, and by the end of the day it appeared to me that she might actually have an appetite for cow work.

The harder I pushed her, the more I demanded of her, the more she seemed to like it. She was wet and tired, but excited and ready to go again. She had passed all her tests and had won a spot on our ranch as a cowhorse.

I was mighty proud. At that time, you could expect to pay $2000 for a good using horse. At $650 she had been a heck of a bargain—just as Alan Randall had predicted.

After we had penned the last bunch of cattle, one of the cowboys looked her over with a critical eye and said, "Any time you want to get your money back on that mare, give me a holler."

Nope. Sabalita had found herself a home.

John Erickson and Snips drag a big calf to the branding fire.
Working the ground (L to R): Scot Erickson, Bobby Barnett,
and Mark Erickson (1996)

Snips

In March 1992, Kris and the kids and I were horseback in Picket Canyon. While we were out, the weather changed suddenly and we got caught in a squall that began as rain and then turned into a vicious little hail storm.

Horses don't enjoy hail storms. The roar and the stinging pellets of ice frighten them. Before we could get back to the barn, Kris's horse ran off with her and dumped her on the ground.

That's when I began looking around for a horse with a slow, easy-going disposition, one I could trust with my wife or kids or visitors to the ranch. Those horses are called "bulletproof" and they're not easy to find. As the saying goes, "Good horses aren't for sale."

But I put out the word to some horse people in Perryton, and a few weeks later we got a call from a lady in Canadian. She had a red dun Quarter Horse that she thought would work for us, and she wanted to find a good home for him. At twelve years old, he was gentle, experienced, calm, and most important, honest. They called him Snips.

We drove to Canadian and gave old Snips a test ride. He was a much bigger horse than the Arabians we were accustomed to riding, with a heavy chest and hindquarter, a thick neck, a long face and big sleepy eyes. He had the quiet disposition we wanted, so I bought him.

For the next couple of years, I seldom had occasion to ride Snips. I was always riding broncs and colts, and didn't feel I could afford the luxury of riding a finished horse.

We used him strictly as a dude horse. When we had kids or inexperienced riders on the ranch, we put them on old Snippers, and he always took good care of them. It wasn't long before my kids refused to ride him. "He's too slow," they said. They wanted to ride our little Arabians that had more flash and fire.

The real problem, of course, was that Snips had been tagged as a dude horse, and the kids no longer considered themselves dudes.

I tried to tell them that Snips was probably a whole lot better horse than we knew, that he was just doing the job we had assigned him. I had always suspected that, but didn't know it for sure until the spring of 1996. We gathered the Mesa pasture and had to brand a little bunch of late calves.

I rode my Nocona mare for the roundup, but decided to heel and drag the calves on Snips, just to see how he would do. I had a feeling that he had been roped on before and that his thick muscular build would make him an excellent mount in a branding pen.

Sure enough, he responded to the challenge. He was alert and responsive, and yes, he sure could drag a heavy load.

All went well until the next-to-last calf, when I discovered that old lazy Snips had quite a bit more fire in him than I had supposed. The way to light him up was to get a rope caught under his tail.

I heeled the calf, dallied, and turned Snips toward the branding fire. I didn't see the calf dart to the left, and the next thing I knew, Snips had the rope under his tail and he was *bucking*, of all things. He bucked into the welded pipe fence and gave my left leg a pretty bad smashing.

I grabbed the top of the fence and let Snips have the rope, the calf, the saddle, and all the rest, while I hobbled around and checked out the damage. (Just bruises).

It was a circus there for a while. My dally turned into a hard-and-fast knot around the horn, and Snips and that feisty heifer calf had to sort things out for themselves. They did. The calf ended up on the ground, with some help from Scot Erickson and Bobby Barnett, and Snips rearranged the rope so that it was pulling on the horn instead of on his tail section.

The dust cloud moved away and we finished the branding.

I had a little trouble getting my left boot off that evening, and for the next several days my left ankle looked like purple bread dough. Otherwise, things turned out pretty well.

I was right about Snips. There was more horse inside that slow-moving body than we had ever suspected. There was also a dark side to Snip's mind. My wife put it well when she said, "Snips is a naughty horse."

At the root of his naughtiness was his compulsion to walk across cattle guards. As you may know, a cattle guard is a device made of pipe and set over a pit. Most cattle and horses respect a cattle guard and won't venture out on those pipes, for fear that their feet and legs will fall into the pit.

Thus, a cattle guard takes the place of a wire gate that has to be opened and closed every time you drive from one pasture to another. Cattle guards are a tremendous convenience, and we have a dozen of them on this ranch.

Snips could walk every stinking one of them. I guess his hooves were big enough so that he could step across without falling through.

This was a minor annoyance until the winter of 1998. Kris had paid a man to put in a lawn in front of the house, and it was a variety of grass that stayed green through the winter. For several days, we noticed Snips standing on the other side of the fence, looking at her grass. The grass in the horse pasture was brown and dormant, and this was the only green grass on the ranch.

Never mind that I was feeding the horses good bright alfalfa hay every day. That wasn't good enough for Snips. He couldn't resist eating my wife's lawn.

The first time we caught him in the yard, I rushed out and fired several shotgun blasts over his head. He scurried back across the cattle guard, a chastened horse, and the experience taught him a valuable lesson. He stopped sneaking in during daylight hours and started coming in the middle of the night.

The next morning, we would find no Snips in the yard, only his droppings and huge hoofprints. One night Kris heard him. He had gone around to the back of the house and was eating dog food out of the self-feeder. (Our three mutts cowered under my pickup while this robbery was in progress, and didn't even make a squeak).

Kris woke me up. I rushed out and fired several blasts into the air. I heard the thief sprinting away, and hoped this would discourage him from coming back. It didn't.

At that point, I had to take drastic action. I loaded him up in the stock trailer and hauled him over to the far west pasture, two miles and four cattle guards away from the scent of my wife's lawn. That worked for three weeks, and then one morning he was back in the yard.

This time I hauled him over to the Flowers place, sixteen miles from the house, and there he stayed—a horse in exile, living amongst dull-witted cows. He misses his old pals from the horse pasture, and that's sure too bad.

He should have thought of that when I was out on the porch in my underwear, firing a shotgun into the frigid darkness. Snips *was* a naughty horse, and he paid the price for it.

John Erickson saddles up Nocona for some cow work (1998)

Nocona

When we bought Nocona in December 1991, I never dreamed she would make a cowhorse. If I had been shopping for a cowhorse, I wouldn't have chosen one that was so—*cute.*

Kathryn Paul had raised her on the Silver Pump ranch in Lipscomb County, and everyone agreed that she would be just perfect for Ashley, our thirteen year old daughter. At the age of three, Nocona was a beautiful dappled-gray Arabian mare. She was petite, graceful, elegant, and had a classic Arabian head with big intelligent eyes.

It seemed a perfect match, a pretty little mare for a pretty little girl.

But after we took her home and rode her for a few months, I began to wonder. First she bucked off Scot, our oldest, at the LZ Ranch spring branding. Then she jumped out from under Ashley a couple of times, dumping her on the ground. After the second dumping, which cracked Ashley's wrist, she lost interest in her little mare.

That's when I began to suspect that Nocona might be more than cute. I hadn't ridden her enough to know what she could do, so I decided to put some miles on her myself. In August 1992 I helped Henry Hale gather some bulls out of a rough canyon pasture north of the Canadian River. These were gentle bulls and I figured it would be a good learning experience for the young mare.

We had no trouble gathering three of the bulls, but the fourth had decided to homestead the cedar forest around Indian Springs, and he was determined not to leave. What began as an easy-going cattle drive turned into a wild ride up and down the caprock, through cedar breaks and mesquite thickets, over rocks and deep washouts.

And there I was, mounted on a little mare I had bought as a kid horse. I rode her so hard that we lost the saddle blanket in the chase, so hard that she was dripping sweat, and my legs were rubbed raw. Through it all, she never stumbled and she never gave up. The harder I pushed her, the more she gave. When the bull turned and charged us, she stepped out of the way and went right back into the fight.

When I pulled off the saddle that evening, I had acquired a new respect for Nocona. She didn't *look* like a cowhorse, but by George, she sure performed like one. She had athletic ability and more guts than any horse I'd ridden in years.

The next spring, I went over to Lipscomb County to help the Bussard family gather and brand on the Heart Ranch. I took Nocona instead of my roping horse, figuring that Lance Bussard and Lane Hill, both fine ropers, would do all the heeling and dragging. I was shocked when Lance said, "John, get your mare."

I had never heeled a calf on Nocona. I didn't know if she could pull a load or not. I had ridden other Arabians that didn't have much appetite for dragging calves. After pulling twenty or twenty-five calves to the branding fire, they would start pointing towards the stock trailer, as if to say, "Look, buster, we're Arabians and this hauling business is for Quarter Horses that weigh 1300 pounds."

Nocona weighed about 850, I would guess, and the calves we had to rope were big. Well, there was only one way to find out. I pulled down the cinches and led Nocona into the branding pen. When she heard the roar of the propane branding heater, I thought she might jump the fence and head for home, but I managed to talk her out of that.

There were forty-five calves in this bunch and I had supposed that Lance would use two heelers. That would have been fine with me. If I had trouble with Nocona, the other man could keep the crew busy and take some of the pressure off of me and my little mare.

I waited for Lance to call another roper. He didn't. When the irons were hot, he gave me a nod and circled his hand in the air, which meant, "Bring the calves."

Nocona was nervous at first, but probably not as nervous as I. When the slack went out of the rope on our first calf, when she felt that first jerk, she staggered sideways and I thought, "Oh boy, here I am in front of my cowboy peers, trying to do a man's work on a kid's horse."

She stumbled around, gained her feet, leaned into the rope, and sledded the calf to the fire.

On the next one, she didn't stumble. She was prepared for the jerk and moved into it. The more calves we dragged, the more she learned, the harder she pulled, and the more she seemed to enjoy the work. We dragged all forty-five calves. I was amazed.

When I got home that night, I said to Ashley, "You know that cute little mare of yours? She just became my number one cowhorse, and you can ride Calypso or Snips."

It worked out all right. By then, Ashley had discovered boys. And I had discovered that the size of a horse is the size of its heart. That cute little mare had a heart as big as a watermelon.

Windsong

Every six months or so, I drive over to the Silver Pump ranch in Lipscomb County to see what horses Kathryn Paul might be interested in selling. Kathryn and I share an enthusiasm for horses of the desert—Arabians—and over the years I have bought several from her.

One day in 1993, we were looking at a group of eight or ten horses that stayed in a pasture south of her house. I pointed to a gray mare that caught my eye. "What about that one?" The mare was a beauty, a classic piece of Arabian horseflesh with the dished face, curved neck, proud tail carriage, and big intelligent eyes.

Kathryn said that was Windsong, a full sister to Nocona, a mare I had bought several years ago. Nocona was a good mare, and if Windsong was a full sister, I wanted to buy her. Then came the bad news. Kathryn had already promised to sell her to a ranch woman in New Mexico.

Several years passed and I forgot about Windsong. Then in the fall of 1997, Kathryn called and said the lady in New Mexico was

161

retiring and wanted to find good homes for her horses. Was I still interested in buying Windsong?

The mare had received some early training but hadn't been ridden much. Kathryn thought she would make a good horse. I said I would take her.

Kathryn and her husband Wayne delivered the mare several weeks later. When she came out of the trailer, I didn't recognize her. She was mature now, a full-grown mare of seven or eight. I remembered her as dappled blue-gray, a common color in young Arabians. Those blue-gray Arabians usually turn white as they get older, and that had been the case with Windsong. She was white and well muscled and bigger than I had expected. She had clearly outgrown her sister Nocona.

Kathryn cautioned me that Windsong hadn't been ridden in years and she wasn't sure how she would respond to being under saddle again, so I handled her as though she were a bronc. I trailered her down to the sand draw and took her through a series of steps that would give me a reading on who she was and what was on her mind.

My reading confirmed what Kathryn had told me, that the mare had received good training as a colt but hadn't been ridden much after that. After three or four sessions in the sand draw, I had her figured out. She was mature, not silly or nervous like a colt. She had a friendly disposition and was plenty smart. She had a good soft mouth and showed no interest in trying to buck.

The only flaws I found in her were that she seemed a little nervous about being in a trailer, and occasionally she would lunge back and fight a halter rope when she was tied solid. Those were minor problems we could work out in time. On the whole, she was everything I had hoped for.

One morning I loaded her into the trailer and noticed that she was uneasy. She went to the front and turned around. That wasn't a good habit and I decided to address it on the spot. As usual, I was working alone. And in a hurry.

I led her out of the trailer, then in again, only this time I led her up to the front and tied the lead rope to the trailer, so that she couldn't turn around. I was about to slip past her and exit the trailer, but instead of moving to the side and letting me pass, she moved backwards and hit the end of the lead rope.

She reared up and fought the rope, then lunged forward and hit me, knocking me into the side of the trailer and down to my knees. In that instant, I remembered a story Lawrence Ellzey had told me about the Yoakley girl.

Back in the early 1950s there was a young woman who lived on a ranch near Canadian, Texas. She was an expert horsewoman and had done well competing in amateur rodeos.

She had a fine horse and the two of them had traveled thousands of miles together. They had a special rapport. But one day Miss Yoakley got into the trailer with the horse, the animal spooked at something, and Miss Yoakley was trampled to death.

It was a terrible tragedy and nobody could understand how it happened. The horse and the girl knew each other *so well*.

And there I was, alone in the trailer with a mare I hardly knew.

Lucky for me, Windsong was a sensible mare and didn't panic. With trembling fingers, I untied the lead rope and got us out of there. A few minutes later I repeated the exercise, but this time I opened the escape door on the side, which is what I should have done in the first place.

It was my fault, not the fault of the mare. I thought I knew everything about the mare, and thought I was horseman enough to deal with whatever came up. I was wrong. The Yoakley girl had been just as wrong, but not as lucky.

I continued riding Windsong over the fall and winter months. It appeared that her main problem was one I had encountered with most of my Arabians—she had to be slowed down and taught to concentrate on cattle work. I am no expert on horse training and have only my experience on the ranch to inform my opinions, but it seems to me that Arabians are not as quick to catch on to cattle work as Quarter Horses.

This may be a genetic disposition. The Quarter Horse was created and bred specifically for ranch work, while the original Arabians were used as war horses by Bedouin tribesmen. They have an exuberance that suited them well for warfare in the desert, but it doesn't transfer immediately to the slower, more directed work on a cattle ranch.

What the Quarter Horse receives through inheritance, the Arabian must learn through experience. They can and do learn it, but it often takes time and patience. Once they have learned to focus on specific tasks, I don't think you can beat them for ranch work, for then the other qualities of the breed come into play.

They are the toughest little beasts you can imagine, and they never have problems with their hooves, feet, or legs. Or so it has been in my experience.

I was in no hurry to make a cowhorse out of Windsong. I had other horses to ride when I needed a proven performer or had a specific task, such as dragging calves at a branding or roping stock in the pasture. My plan was to bring her along slowly, and start roping off her in the spring of 1999.

In May of '98 I rode her when we rounded up our East Pasture. This was a gentle bunch of cattle, and I thought it would be slow, easy work, just right for a green horse. But as we were moving the herd, a young calf bolted away and headed north in a dead run.

Among bovines, this is irrational behavior. Cattle are naturally inclined to go *towards* and stay *with* other cattle. When a young calf bolts the herd, it is likely to run until it drops, which may be miles away from the herd and its mother.

This calf was on a course that would take it up into Point Creek Canyon, one of the deepest and roughest canyons on the ranch. Once in that canyon, the calf would be lost, alone, and virtually impossible to find.

I happened to be the rider closest to the calf when it broke the herd, and I gave chase. I had never ridden Windsong hard over such rough country. I didn't want to pull the throttle, but I had to. We caught up with the calf and tried to turn him back to the herd. He wouldn't turn. Someone would have to rope him.

I glanced over my shoulder, hoping to see another cowboy coming with a loaded rope. I saw Brent Clapp, but he was chasing a second calf that had quit the herd. I had never thrown a rope off Windsong and had no idea how she would respond to it. I was fixing to find out. I had no choice.

I built a loop and pointed Windsong at the calf. I held my fire until we passed through some broken country and came to a little flat. The mare rated the calf and gave me an easy shot. I mailed it to the right address, dallied up, and brought the calf to a stop, wondering if the mare would spook and start bucking at this strange object on the rope.

She performed as though she had been doing this all her life. At that point, we scrapped the training program. Windsong had just worked herself into a steady job.